The Poems

of

Alfred Lord Tennyson

BLACK'S READERS SERVICE COMPANY

NEW YORK, N. Y.

CONTENTS

INTRODUCTION

That sons delight in casting down the idols of their fathers is a commonplace of history, and nowhere is this truth more boldly scrawled than across the story of the arts. In no other portion of our human records can the chronicle of ceaseless warfare between youth and age be read more clearly. Almost every generation of writers, painters and musicians rises in instinctive rebellion against the immediately preceding generation and all its works, while exalting more ancient ideals, or straining towards a future whose ideals are as yet but vaguely defined and most bewildering to the average man who, according to his own confession, knows nothing of art but knows only what he likes. We have ourselves witnessed one of the most violent of these revolts: the revolt against Victorian art; a revolt that was conducted with all the more ferocity and confidence because the embattled artists found themselves companioned by a larger public that laughed at or denounced Victorianism in all its forms. Only recently have enough years elapsed, since the end of the longest reign in English history, for time to perform its characteristic function of clarifying distant objects; only lately have we come to realize that there were many mansions in the house of the good Queen, and that a blanket condemnation of "Victorianism" is a little sillier than anything it might condemn. We have begun to discriminate and select, and with discrimination the possibility of admiration has returned.

It was natural that Tennyson should receive rather more than an average share of the ridicule and disapproval heaped upon the Victorians, for among them all he was perhaps the most lavishly and injudiciously praised. In an age that specialized in hero-worship, he was at once hero *par excellence* and victim. Rogers informed the public that Shakespeare himself could not have bettered "Locksley Hall"; and Poe announced: "In perfect sincerity I regard Alfred Tennyson as the noblest poet that ever lived." Flattered and spoiled as he was by the friends of his youth, the pontifical Laureate was still more spoiled and flattered by the great world in his age. "When," as the late Sir Edmund Gosse remarked, "a very clever man like the late Duke of Argyll, a man of sober years, could say, without being reproached, that Tennyson's blank verse in the 'Idylls' was sweeter and stronger than 'the stately march of Elizabethan English in its golden prime'; when Mr. Gladstone could declare of Arthur in the same 'Idylls' that 'he knew not where to look in history or letters for a nobler or more overpowering conception of man as he might be,' then a reaction, however tenderly delayed, was inevitable."

But it was not merely the excessive praise accorded an individual poet that gave impetus and strength to the reaction against Tennyson; it was his perfect identification with his age. Even in the matter of dates that identification was singularly accurate. He was born less than ten years before his Queen, and she outlived him by a little more than eight years. When he first saw the light, at the Rectory of Somersby in Lincolnshire, it was the year 1809; the year of the Peace of Vienna and of the Battle of Talavera. When the full moonlight shone upon his strong, dead face at Aldworth, it was the year 1892; the year of the great coal miners' strike in England, and of the Homestead strike in the United States. Beneath the vast social structure that the Victorian world had thought so sound, dark forces were thrusting upward; timbers were creaking, masonry was crumbling here and there. Tennyson's rise as a poet had corresponded with the expansion of British trade, with the increase of British wealth, with the crystallization of the Victorian ideal of life,—"that ideal so noble in intention, so conveniently limited in application, so guarded in its holiness." When he came to the midway station of his journey, he did not find himself like Dante in a dark wood, but on an illumined height; for in 1850, the year of his marriage and of "In Memoriam," he was named Poet Laureate. In a little more than forty years he had achieved eminence; for a little more than forty years he would be, to the great public, an oracle speaking from a mountain, while at Farringford and Aldworth he and his wife and children would incarnate the golden virtues of Victorian domesticity. (At Farringford, on the Isle of Wight, the atmosphere then engendered lingers still; for to visit it, as I did a month or so ago, is to walk into the past.) For a little more than forty years he would be the guardian priest of British culture and morality; he would be the almost sacred fount of wisdom from which the upper middle class might drink in certainty of confirmation and consolation. He would preach progress, even liberalism, but assure his congregation there was no hurry:

> This fine old world of ours is but a child
> Yet in the go-cart. Patience! Give it time
> To learn its limbs; there is a hand that guides . . .

And because of this, when the reaction against Victorianism set in, the man would bear the brunt of an attack that was directed at an age.

But the reaction has done its work; and when we no longer ask from Tennyson what his contemporaries asked, it is folly to pick out for condemnation those elements in his writing which aroused their veneration. We no longer turn to him for sociological wisdom, moral infallibility, or religious reassurance. What we ask of him now is not didacticism, but lyricism; not ideas, but poetry; not (following Harold Nicholson's distinction) applied poetry, but pure poetry. And that we find in abundance, for his lyric gift was one of the finest, strongest, and most various that the world has known. Had he been no more than the perfect master of his craft, which he was, contemplation of that mastery would provide an exquisite and pure enjoyment for all who love the craft. But he was more; he was a poet born, whatever the world may have made him as a thinker. "He sang, and since the gift of song is given to every nightingale, and to one man in every fifty years, he had the favour of the gods before which all criticism falls."

BEN RAY REDMAN.

POEMS

THE MUSE

MERLIN AND THE GLEAM

O young Mariner,
You from the haven
Under the sea-cliff,
You that are watching
The gray Magician
With eyes of wonder,
I am Merlin,
And *I* am dying,
I am Merlin
Who follow the Gleam.

Mighty the Wizard
Who found me at sunrise
Sleeping, and woke me
And learn'd me Magic!
Great the Master,
And sweet the Magic,
When over the valley,
In early summers,
Over the mountain,
On human faces,
And all around me,
Moving to melody,
Floated the Gleam.

1

Once at the croak
  of a Raven who crost it,
A barbarous people,
Blind to the magic
And deaf to the melody,
Snarl'd at and cursed me.
A demon vext me,
The light retreated,
The landskip darken'd,
The melody deaden'd,
The Master whisper'd,
'Follow the Gleam.'

Then to the melody,
Over a wilderness
Gliding, and glancing at
Elf of the woodland,
Gnome of the cavern,
Griffin and Giant,
And dancing of Fairies
In desolate hollows,
And wraiths of the mountain
And rolling of dragons
By warble of water,
Or cataract music
Of falling torrents,
Flitted the Gleam.

Down from the mountain
And over the level,
And streaming and shining on
Silent river,
Silvery willow,

Pasture and plowland,
Innocent maidens,
Garrulous children,
Homestead and harvest,
Reaper and gleaner,
And rough-ruddy faces
Of lowly labor,
Slided the Gleam—

Then, with a melody
Stronger and statelier,
Led me at length
To the city and palace
Of Arthur the King;
Touch'd at the golden
Cross of the churches,
Flash'd on the tournament,
Flicker'd and bicker'd
From helmet to helmet,
And last on the forehead
Of Arthur the blameless
Rested the Gleam.

Clouds and darkness
Closed upon Camelot;
Arthur had vanish'd
I knew not whither,
The king who loved me,
And cannot die;
For out of the darkness
Silent and slowly
The Gleam, that had waned
  to a wintry glimmer

On icy fallow
And faded forest,
Drew to the valley
Named of the shadow,
And slowly brightening
Out of the glimmer,
And slowly moving again
 to a melody
Yearningly tender,
Fell on the shadow,
No longer a shadow,
But clothed with the Gleam.

And broader and brighter
The Gleam flying onward,
Wed to the melody,
Sang thro' the world;
And slower and fainter,
Old and weary,
But eager to follow,
I saw, whenever
In passing it glanced upon
Hamlet or city,
That under the Crosses
The dead man's garden,
The mortal hillock,
Would break into blossom.
And so to the land's
Last limit I came—
And can no longer,
But die rejoicing,
For thro' the Magic
Of Him the Mighty,

Who taught me in childhood,
There on the border
Of boundless Ocean,
And all but in Heaven
Hovers the Gleam.

Not of the sunlight,
Not of the moonlight,
Not of the starlight!
O young Mariner,
Down to the haven,
Call your companions,
Launch your vessel
And crowd your canvas,
And, ere it vanishes
Over the margin,
After it, follow it,
Follow the Gleam.

THE SEA

THE KRAKEN

Below the thunders of the upper deep,
Far, far beneath in the abysmal sea,
His ancient, dreamless, uninvaded sleep
The Kraken sleepeth: faintest sunlights flee
About his shadowy sides; above him swell
Huge sponges of millennial growth and height;
And far away into the sickly light,
From many a wondrous grot and secret cell
Unnumber'd and enormous polypi
Winnow with giant arms the slumbering green.
There hath he lain for ages, and will lie
Battening upon huge sea-worms in his sleep,
Until the latter fire shall heat the deep;
Then once by man and angels to be seen,
In roaring he shall rise and on the surface die.

THE MERMAN

Who would be
A merman bold,
Sitting alone,
Singing alone
Under the sea,
With a crown of gold,
On a throne?

I would be a merman bold,
I would sit and sing the whole of the day;
I would fill the sea-halls with a voice of power;
But at night I would roam abroad and play
With the mermaids in and out of the rocks,
Dressing their hair with the white sea-flower;
And holding them back by their flowing locks
I would kiss them often under the sea,
And kiss them again till they kiss'd me
    Laughingly, laughingly;
And then we would wander away, away,
To the pale-green sea-groves straight and high,
    Chasing each other merrily.

There would be neither moon nor star,
But the wave would make music above us afar—
Low thunder and light in the magic night—
    Neither moon nor star.
We would call aloud in the dreamy dells,
Call to each other and whoop and cry
    All night, merrily, merrily.
They would pelt me with starry spangles and shells,
Laughing and clapping their hands between,
    All night, merrily, merrily,
But I would throw to them back in mine
Turkis and agate and almondine;
Then leaping out upon them unseen
I would kiss them often under the sea,
And kiss them again till they kiss'd me
    Laughingly, laughingly.
O, what a happy life were mine
Under the hollow-hung ocean green!
Soft are the moss-beds under the sea;
We would live merrily, merrily.

THE MERMAID

Who would be,
A mermaid fair,
Singing alone,
Combing her hair
Under the sea,
In a golden curl
With a comb of pearl,
On a throne?

I would be a mermaid fair;
I would sing to myself the whole of the day;
With a comb of pearl I would comb my hair;
And still as I comb'd I would sing and say,
'Who is it loves me? who loves not me?'
I would comb my hair till my ringlets would fall
     Low adown, low adown,
From under my starry sea-bud crown
     Low adown and around,
And I should look like a fountain of gold
       Springing alone
   With a shrill inner sound,
       Over the throne
   In the midst of the hall;
Till that great sea-snake under the sea
From his coiled sleeps in the central deeps
Would slowly trail himself sevenfold
Round the hall where I sate, and look in at the gate
With his large calm eyes for the love of me.
And all the mermen under the sea
Would feel their immortality
Die in their hearts for the love of me.

But at night I would wander away, away,
  I would fling on each side my low-flowing locks,
And lightly vault from the throne and play
  With the mermen in and out of the rocks;
We would run to and fro, and hide and seek,
  On the broad seawolds in the crimson shells,
Whose silvery spikes are nighest the sea.
But if any came near I would call, and shriek,
And adown the steep like a wave I would leap
  From the diamond-ledges that jut from the dells;
For I would not be kiss'd by all who would list
Of the bold merry mermen under the sea.
They would sue me, and woo me, and flatter me,
In the purple twilights under the sea;
But the king of them all would carry me,
Woo me, and win me, and marry me,
In the branching jaspers under the sea.
Then all the dry pied things that be
In the hueless mosses under the sea
Would curl round my silver feet silently,
All looking up for the love of me.
And if I should carol aloud, from aloft
All things that are forked, and horned, and soft
Would lean out from the hollow sphere of the sea,
All looking down for the love of me.

THE SAILOR BOY

  HE ROSE at dawn and, fired with hope,
    Shot o'er the seething harbor-bar,
  And reach'd the ship and caught the rope,
    And whistled to the morning star.

And while he whistled long and loud
  He heard a fierce mermaiden cry,
'O boy, tho' thou art young and proud,
  I see the place where thou wilt lie.

'The sands and yeasty surges mix
  In caves about the dreary bay,
And on thy ribs the limpet sticks,
  And in thy heart the scrawl shall play.'

'Fool,' he answer'd, 'death is sure
  To those that stay and those that roam,
But I will nevermore endure
  To sit with empty hands at home.

'My mother clings about my neck,
  My sisters crying, "Stay for shame;"
My father raves of death and wreck,—
  They are all to blame, they are all to blame.

'God help me! save I take my part
  Of danger on the roaring sea,
A devil rises in my heart,
  Far worse than any death to me.'

THE ISLET

'WHITHER, O whither, love, shall we go,
For a score of sweet little summers or so?'
The sweet little wife of the singer said,
On the day that follow'd the day she was wed,
'Whither, O whither, love, shall we go?'
And the singer shaking his curly head

Turn'd as he sat, and struck the keys
There at his right with a sudden crash,
Singing, 'And shall it be over the seas
With a crew that is neither rude nor rash,
But a bevy of Eroses apple-cheek'd,
In a shallop of crystal ivory-beak'd?
With a satin sail of a ruby glow,
To a sweet little Eden on earth that I know,
A mountain islet pointed and peak'd;
Waves on a diamond shingle dash,
Cataract brooks to the ocean run,
Fairily-delicate palaces shine
Mixt with myrtle and clad with vine,
And overstream'd and silvery-streak'd
With many a rivulet high against the sun
The facets of the glorious mountain flash
Above the valleys of palm and pine.'

'Thither, O thither, love, let us go.'

'No, no, no!
For in all that exquisite isle, my dear,
There is but one bird with a musical throat,
And his compass is but of a single note,
That it makes one weary to hear.'

'Mock me not! mock me not! love, let us go.'

'No, love, no.
For the bud ever breaks into bloom on the tree,
And a storm never wakes on the lonely sea,
And a worm is there in the lonely wood,
That pierces the liver and blackens the blood,
And makes it a sorrow to be.'

'BREAK, BREAK, BREAK'

BREAK, break, break,
  On thy cold gray stones, O Sea!
And I would that my tongue could utter
  The thoughts that arise in me.

O, well for the fisherman's boy,
  That he shouts with his sister at play!
O, well for the sailor lad,
  That he sings in his boat on the bay!

And the stately ships go on
  To their haven under the hill;
But O for the touch of a vanish'd hand,
  And the sound of a voice that is still!

Break, break, break,
  At the foot of thy crags, O Sea!
But the tender grace of a day that is dead
  Will never come back to me.

BALLADS

ORIANA

MY HEART is wasted with my woe,
            Oriana.
There is no rest for me below,
            Oriana.
When the long dun wolds are ribb'd with snow,
And loud the Norland whirlwinds blow,
Alone I wander to and fro,
            Oriana.

Ere the light on dark was growing,
            Oriana,
At midnight the cock was crowing,
            Oriana;
Winds were blowing, waters flowing,
We heard the steeds to battle going,
Aloud the hollow bugle blowing,
            Oriana.

In the yew-wood black as night,
            Oriana,
Ere I rode into the fight,
            Oriana,
While blissful tears blinded my sight
By star-shine and by moonlight,
I to thee my troth did plight,
            Oriana.

13

She stood upon the castle wall,
>> Oriana;
She watch'd my crest among them all,
>> Oriana;
She saw me fight, she heard me call,
When forth there stept a foeman tall,
Atween me and the castle wall,
>> Oriana.

The bitter arrow went aside,
>> Oriana;
The false, false arrow went aside,
>> Oriana;
The damned arrow glanced aside,
And pierced thy heart, my love, my bride,
Thy heart, my life, my love, my bride,
>> Oriana!

O, narrow, narrow was the space,
>> Oriana!
Loud, loud rung out the bugle's brays,
>> Oriana.
O, deathful stabs were dealt apace,
The battle deepen'd in its place,
But I was down upon my face,
>> Oriana.

They should have stabb'd me where I lay,
>> Oriana!
How could I rise and come away,
>> Oriana?
How could I look upon the day?

They should have stabb'd me where I lay,
They should have trod me into clay,
      Oriana.

O breaking heart that will not break,
      Oriana!
O pale, pale face so sweet and meek,
      Oriana!
Thou smilest, but thou dost not speak,
And then the tears run down my cheek,
What wantest thou? whom dost thou seek,
      Oriana?

I cry aloud; none hear my cries,
      Oriana.
Thou comest atween me and the skies,
      Oriana.
I feel the tears of blood arise
Up from my heart unto my eyes,
Within thy heart my arrow lies,
      Oriana.

O cursed hand! O cursed blow,
      Oriana!
O happy thou that liest low,
      Oriana!
All night the silence seems to flow
Beside me in my utter woe,
A weary, weary way I go,
      Oriana!

When Norland winds pipe down the sea,
      Oriana,
I walk, I dare not think of thee,
      Oriana.

Thou liest beneath the greenwood tree,
I dare not die and come to thee,
I hear the roaring of the sea,
    Oriana.

———

THE LORD OF BURLEIGH

In her ear he whispers gaily,
  'If my heart by signs can tell,
Maiden, I have watch'd thee daily,
  And I think thou lov'st me well.'
She replies, in accents fainter,
  'There is none I love like thee.'
He is but a landscape-painter,
  And a village maiden she.
He to lips that fondly falter
  Presses his without reproof,
Leads her to the village altar,
  And they leave her father's roof.
'I can make no marriage present;
  Little can I give my wife.
Love will make our cottage pleasant,
  And I love thee more than life.'
They by parks and lodges going
  See the lordly castles stand;
Summer woods, about them blowing,
  Made a murmur in the land.
From deep thought himself he rouses,
  Says to her that loves him well,
'Let us see these handsome houses
  Where the wealthy nobles dwell.'

So she goes by him attended,
  Hears him lovingly converse,
Sees whatever fair and splendid
  Lay betwixt his home and hers;
Parks with oak and chestnut shady,
  Parks and order'd gardens great,
Ancient homes of lord and lady,
  Built for pleasure and for state.
All he shows her makes him dearer;
  Evermore she seems to gaze
On that cottage growing nearer,
  Where they twain will spend their days.
O, but she will love him truly!
  He shall have a cheerful home,
She will order all things duly,
  When beneath his roof they come.
Thus her heart rejoices greatly,
  Till a gateway she discerns
With armorial bearings stately,
  And beneath the gate she turns,
Sees a mansion more majestic
  Than all those she saw before.
Many a gallant gay domestic
  Bows before him at the door;
And they speak in gentle murmur,
  When they answer to his call,
While he treads with footstep firmer,
  Leading on from hall to hall.
And, while now she wonders blindly,
  Nor the meaning can divine,
Proudly turns he round and kindly,
  'All of this is mine and thine.'
Here he lives in state and bounty,
  Lord of Burleigh, fair and free:

Not a lord in all the county
  Is so great a lord as he.
All at once the color flushes
  Her sweet face from brow to chin;
As it were with shame she blushes,
  And her spirit changed within.
Then her countenance all over
  Pale again as death did prove;
But he clasp'd her like a lover,
  And he cheer'd her soul with love.
So she strove against her weakness,
  Tho' at times her spirit sank,
Shaped her heart with woman's meekness
  To all duties of her rank;
And a gentle consort made he,
  And her gentle mind was such
That she grew a noble lady,
  And the people loved her much.
But a trouble weigh'd upon her,
  And perplex'd her, night and morn,
With the burthen of an honor
  Unto which she was not born.
Faint she grew, and ever fainter,
  And she murmur'd, 'O, that he
Were once more that landscape-painter
  Which did win my heart from me!'
So she droop'd and droop'd before him,
  Fading slowly from his side;
Three fair children first she bore him,
  Then before her time she died.
Weeping, weeping late and early,
  Walking up and pacing down,
Deeply mourn'd the Lord of Burleigh,
  Burleigh-house by Stamford-town.

And he came to look upon her,
  And he look'd at her and said,
'Bring the dress and put it on her,
  That she wore when she was wed.'
Then her people, softly treading,
  Bore to earth her body, drest
In the dress that she was wed in,
  That her spirit might have rest.

────────

THE SISTERS' SHAME*

WE WERE two daughters of one race;
She was the fairest in the face.
  The wind is blowing in turret and tree.
They were together, and she fell;
Therefore revenge became me well.
  O, the earl was fair to see!

She died; she went to burning flame;
She mix'd her ancient blood with shame.
  The wind is howling in turret and tree.
Whole weeks and months, and early and late,
To win his love I lay in wait.
  O, the earl was fair to see!

I made a feast; I bade him come;
I won his love, I brought him home,
  The wind is roaring in turret and tree.
And after supper on a bed,
Upon my lap he laid his head.
  O, the earl was fair to see!

*Edited under a new title to distinguish it from a later poem.

I kiss'd his eyelids into rest,
His ruddy cheek upon my breast.
   The wind is raging in turret and tree.
I hated him with the hate of hell,
But I loved his beauty passing well.
   O, the earl was fair to see!

I rose up in the silent night;
I made my dagger sharp and bright.
   The wind is raving in turret and tree.
As half-asleep his breath he drew,
Three times I stabb'd him thro' and thro'.
   O, the earl was fair to see!

I curl'd and comb'd his comely head,
He look'd so grand when he was dead.
   The wind is blowing in turret and tree.
I wrapt his body in the sheet,
And laid him at his mother's feet.
   O, the earl was fair to see!

DRAMATIC MONOLOGUES

MAUD

Part I

Section I

I HATE the dreadful hollow behind the little wood;
Its lips in the field above are dabbled with blood-red heath,
The red-ribb'd ledges drip with a silent horror of blood,
And Echo there, whatever is ask'd her, answers "Death."

For there in the ghastly pit long since a body was found,
His who had given me life—O father! O God! was it well?—
Mangled, and flatten'd, and crush'd, and dinted into the
    ground;
There yet lies the rock that fell with him when he fell.

Did he fling himself down? who knows? for a vast speculation
    had fail'd,
And ever he mutter'd and madden'd, and ever wann'd with
    despair,
And out he walk'd when the wind like a broken worldling
    wail'd,
And the flying gold of the ruin'd woodlands drove thro' the
    air.

I remember the time, for the roots of my hair were stirr'd
By a shuffled step, by a dead weight trail'd, by a whisper'd
    fright,
And my pulses closed their gates with a shock on my heart as
    I heard
The shrill-edged shriek of a mother divide the shuddering
    night.

Villainy somewhere! whose? One says, we are villains all.
Not he; his honest fame should at least by me be maintained;
But that old man, now lord of the broad estate and the Hall,
Dropt off gorged from a scheme that had left us flaccid and
    drain'd.

Why do they prate of the blessings of peace? we have made
    them a curse,
Pickpockets, each hand lusting for all that is not its own;
And lust of gain, in the spirit of Cain, is it better or worse
Than the heart of the citizen hissing in war on his own hearth-
    stone?

But these are the days of advance, the works of the men of
    mind,
When who but a fool would have faith in a tradesman's ware
    or his word?
Is it peace or war? Civil war, as I think, and that of a kind
The viler, as underhand, not openly bearing the sword.

Sooner or later I too may passively take the print
Of the golden age—why not? I have neither hope nor trust;
May make my heart as a millstone, set my face as a flint,
Cheat and be cheated, and die—who knows? we are ashes and
    dust.

Peace sitting under her olive, and slurring the days gone by,
When the poor are hovell'd and hustled together, each sex,
 like swine,
When only the ledger lives, and when only not all men lie;
Peace in her vineyard—yes!—but a company forges the wine.

And the vitriol madness flushes up in the ruffian's head,
Till the filthy by-lane rings to the yell of the trampled wife,
And chalk and alum and plaster are sold to the poor for bread.
And the spirit of murder works in the very means of life,

And Sleep must lie down arm'd, for the villainous centre-bits
Grind on the wakeful ear in the hush of the moonless nights,
While another is cheating the sick of a few last gasps, as he
 sits
To pestle a poison'd poison behind his crimson lights.

When a Mammonite mother kills her babe for a burial fee,
And Timour-Mammon grins on a pile of children's bones,
Is it peace or war? better, war! loud war by land and by sea,
War with a thousand battles, and shaking a hundred thrones!

For I trust if an enemy's fleet came yonder round by the hill,
And the rushing battle-bolt sang from the three-decker out of
 the foam,
That the smooth-faced, snub-nosed rogue would leap from his
 counter and till,
And strike, if he could, were it but with his cheating yard-
 wand, home.—

What! am I raging alone as my father raged in his mood?
Must *I* too creep to the hollow and dash myself down and die

Rather than hold by the law that I made, nevermore to brood
On a horror of shatter'd limbs and a wretched swindler's lie?

Would there be sorrow for *me?* there was *love* in the passionate shriek,
Love for the silent thing that had made false haste to the
grave—
Wrapt in a cloak, as I saw him, and thought he would rise and
speak
And rave at the lie and the liar, ah God, as he used to rave.

I am sick of the Hall and the hill, I am sick of the moor and
the main.
Why should I stay? can a sweeter chance ever come to me
here?
O, having the nerves of motion as well as the nerves of pain,
Were it not wise if I fled from the place and the pit and the
fear?

Workmen up at the Hall!—they are coming back from abroad;
The dark old place will be gilt by the touch of a millionaire.
I have heard, I know not whence, of the singular beauty of
Maud;
I play'd with the girl when a child; she promised then to be
fair.

Maud, with her venturous climbings and tumbles and childish
escapes,
Maud, the delight of the village, the ringing joy of the Hall,
Maud, with her sweet purse-mouth when my father dangled
the grapes,
Maud, the beloved of my mother, the moon-faced darling of
all,—

What is she now? My dreams are bad. She may bring me a
curse.

No, there is fatter game on the moor; she will let me alone.

Thanks; for the fiend best knows whether woman or man be
the worse.

I will bury myself in myself, and the Devil may pipe to his
own.

Section II

Long have I sigh'd for a calm; God grant I may find it at last!

It will never be broken by Maud; she has neither savor nor
salt,

But a cold and clear-cut face, as I found when her carriage
past,

Perfectly beautiful; let it be granted her; where is the fault?

All that I saw—for her eyes were downcast, not to be seen—

Faultily faultless, icily regular, splendidly null,

Dead perfection, no more; nothing more, if it had not been

For a chance of travel, a paleness, an hour's defect of the rose,

Or an underlip, you may call it a little too ripe, too full,

Or the least little delicate aquiline curve in a sensitive nose,

From which I escaped heart-free, with the least little touch of
spleen.

Section III

Cold and clear-cut face, why come you so cruelly meek,

Breaking a slumber in which all spleenful folly was drown'd?

Pale with the golden beam of an eyelash dead on the cheek,

Passionless, pale, cold face, star-sweet on a gloom profound;

Womanlike, taking revenge too deep for a transient wrong

Done but in thought to your beauty, and ever as pale as before

Growing and fading and growing upon me without a sound,

Luminous, gemlike, ghostlike, deathlike, half the night long
Growing and fading and growing, till I could bear it no more,
But arose, and all by myself in my own dark garden ground,
Listening now to the tide in its broad-flung shipwrecking roar,
Now to the scream of a madden'd beach dragg'd down by the
  wave,
Walk'd in a wintry wind by a ghastly glimmer, and found
The shining daffodil dead, and Orion low in his grave.

Section IV

A million emeralds break from the ruby-budded lime
In the little grove where I sit—ah, wherefore cannot I be
Like things of the season gay, like the bountiful season bland,
When the far-off sail is blown by the breeze of a softer clime,
Half-lost in the liquid azure bloom of a crescent of sea,
The silent sapphire-spangled marriage ring of the land?

Below me, there, is the village, and looks how quiet and small!
And yet bubbles o'er like a city, with gossip, scandal, and
  spite;
And Jack on his ale-house bench has as many lies as a Czar;
And here on the landward side, by a red rock, glimmers the
  Hall;
And up in the high Hall-garden I see her pass like a light;
But sorrow seize me if ever that light be my leading star!

When have I bow'd to her father, the wrinkled head of the
  race?
I met her to-day with her brother, but not to her brother I
  bow'd;
I bow'd to his lady-sister as she rode by on the moor,
But the fire of a foolish pride flash'd over her beautiful face.

O child, you wrong your beauty, believe it, in being so proud;
Your father has wealth well-gotten, and I am nameless and
poor.

I keep but a man and a maid, ever ready to slander and steal;
I know it, and smile a hard-set smile, like a stoic, or like
A wiser epicurean, and let the world have its way
For nature is one with rapine, a harm no preacher can heal;
The Mayfly is torn by the swallow, the sparrow spear'd by the
shrike,
And the whole little wood where I sit is a world of plunder
and prey.

We are puppets, Man in his pride, and Beauty fair in her
flower;
Do we move ourselves, or are moved by an unseen hand at a
game
That pushes us off from the board, and others ever succeed?
Ah yet, we cannot be kind to each other here for an hour;
We whisper, and hint, and chuckle, and grin at a brother's
shame;
However we brave it out, we men are a little breed.

A monstrous eft was of old the lord and master of earth,
For him did his high sun flame, and his river billowing ran,
And he felt himself in his force to be Nature's crowning race.
As nine months go to the shaping an infant ripe for his birth,
So many a million of ages have gone to the making of man:
He now is first, but is he the last? is he not too base?

The man of science himself is fonder of glory, and vain,
An eye well-practised in nature, a spirit bounded and poor;
The passionate heart of the poet is whirl'd into folly and vice.
I would not marvel at either, but keep a temperate brain;

For not to desire or admire, if a man could learn it, were more
Than to walk all day like the sultan of old in a garden of
    spice.

For the drift of the Maker is dark, an Isis hid by the veil.
Who knows the ways of the world, how God will bring them
    about?
Our planet is one, the suns are many, the world is wide.
Shall I weep if a Poland fall? shall I shriek if a Hungary fail?
Or an infant civilization be ruled with rod or with knout?
I have not made the world, and He that made it will guide.

Be mine a philosopher's life in the quiet woodland ways,
Where if I cannot be gay let a passionless peace be my lot,
Far-off from the clamor of liars belied in the hubbub of lies;
From the long-neck'd geese of the world that are ever hissing
    dispraise
Because their natures are little, and, whether he heed it or not,
Where each man walks with his head in a cloud of poisonous
    flies.

And most of all would I flee from the cruel madness of love,
The honey of poison-flowers and all the measureless ill.
Ah, Maud, you milk-white fawn, you are all unmeet for a wife.
Your mother is mute in her grave as her image in marble
    above;
Your father is ever in London, you wander about at your will;
You have but fed on the roses and lain in the lilies of life.

SECTION V

A voice by the cedar tree
In the meadow under the Hall!
She is singing an air that is known to me,
A passionate ballad gallant and gay,

A martial song like a trumpet's call!
Singing alone in the morning of life,
In the happy morning of life and of May,
Singing of men that in battle array,
Ready in heart and ready in hand,
March with banner and bugle and fife
To the death, for their native land.

Maud with her exquisite face,
And wild voice pealing up to the sunny sky,
And feet like sunny gems on an English green,
Maud in the light of her youth and her grace,
Singing of Death, and of Honor that cannot die,
Till I well could weep for a time so sordid and mean,
And myself so languid and base.

Silence, beautiful voice!
Be still, for you only trouble the mind
With a joy in which I cannot rejoice,
A glory I shall not find.
Still! I will hear you no more,
For your sweetness hardly leaves me a choice
But to move to the meadow and fall before
Her feet on the meadow grass, and adore,
Not her, who is neither courtly nor kind,
Not her, not her, but a voice.

Section VI

Morning arises stormy and pale,
No sun, but a wannish glare
In fold upon fold of hueless cloud;
And the budded peaks of the wood are bow'd,
Caught, and cuff'd by the gale:
I had fancied it would be fair.

Whom but Maud should I meet
Last night, when the sunset burn'd
On the blossom'd gable-ends
At the head of the village street,
Whom but Maud should I meet?
And she touch'd my hand with a smile so sweet,
She made me divine amends
For a courtesy not return'd.

And thus a delicate spark
Of glowing and growing light
Thro' the livelong hours of the dark
Kept itself warm in the heart of my dreams,
Ready to burst in a color'd flame;
Till at last, when the morning came
In a cloud, it faded, and seems
But an ashen-gray delight.

What if with her sunny hair,
And smile as sunny as cold,
She meant to weave me a snare
Of some coquettish deceit,
Cleopatra-like as of old
To entangle me when we met,
To have her lion roll in a silken net
And fawn at a victor's feet.

Ah, what shall I be at fifty
Should Nature keep me alive,
If I find the world so bitter
When I am but twenty-five?
Yet, if she were not a cheat,
If Maud were all that she seem'd,
And her smile were all that I dream'd.

Then the world were not so bitter
But a smile could make it sweet.

What if, tho' her eye seem'd full
Of a kind intent to me,
What if that dandy-despot, he,
That jewell'd mass of millinery,
That oil'd and curl'd Assyrian bull
Smelling of musk and of insolence,
Her brother, from whom I keep aloof,
Who wants the finer politic sense
To mask, tho' but in his own behoof,
With a glassy smile his brutal scorn—
What if he had told her yestermorn
How prettily for his own sweet sake
A face of tenderness might be feign'd,
And a moist mirage in desert eyes,
That so, when the rotten hustings shake
In another month to his brazen lies,
A wretched vote may be gain'd?

For a raven ever croaks, at my side,
Keep watch and ward, keep watch and ward,
Or thou wilt prove their tool.
Yea, too, myself from myself I guard,
For often a man's own angry pride
Is cap and bells for a fool.

Perhaps the smile and tender tone
Came out of her pitying womanhood,
For am I not, am I not, here alone
So many a summer since she died,
My mother, who was so gentle and good?
Living alone in an empty house,

Here half-hid in the gleaming wood,
Where I hear the dead at midday moan,
And the shrieking rush of the wainscot mouse,
And my own sad name in corners cried,
When the shiver of dancing leaves is thrown
About its echoing chambers wide,
Till a morbid hate and horror have grown
Of a world in which I have hardly mixt,
And a morbid eating lichen fixt
On a heart half-turn'd to stone.

O heart of stone, are you flesh, and caught
By that you swore to withstand?
For what was it else within me wrought
But, I fear, the new strong wine of love,
That made my tongue to stammer and trip
When I saw the treasured splendor, her hand,
Come sliding out of her sacred glove,
And the sunlight broke from her lip?

I have play'd with her when a child;
She remembers it now we meet.
Ah, well, well, well, I *may* be beguiled
By some coquettish deceit.
Yet, if she were not a cheat,
If Maud were all that she seem'd,
And her smile had all that I dream'd,
Then the world were not so bitter
But a smile could make it sweet.

Section VII

Did I hear it half in a doze
    Long since, I know not where?
Did I dream it an hour ago,
    When asleep in this arm-chair?

Men were drinking together,
  Drinking and talking of me:
'Well, if it prove a girl, the boy
  Will have plenty; so let it be.'

Is it an echo of something
  Read with a boy's delight,
Viziers nodding together
  In some Arabian night?

Strange, that I hear two men,
  Somewhere, talking of me:
'Well, if it prove a girl, my boy
  Will have plenty; so let it be.'

SECTION VIII

She came to the village church,
And sat by a pillar alone;
An angel watching an urn
Wept over her, carved in stone;
And once, but once, she lifted her eyes,
And suddenly, sweetly, strangely blush'd
To find they were met by my own;
And suddenly, sweetly, my heart beat stronger
And thicker, until I heard no longer
The snowy-banded, dilettante,
Delicate-handed priest intone;
And thought, is it pride? and mused and sigh'd,
'No surely, now it cannot be pride.'

SECTION IX

I was walking a mile,
More than a mile from the shore,

The sun look'd out with a smile
Betwixt the cloud and the moor;
And riding at set of day
Over the dark moor land,
Rapidly riding far away,
She waved to me with her hand.
There were two at her side,
Something flash'd in the sun,
Down by the hill I saw them ride,
In a moment they were gone;
Like a sudden spark
Struck vainly in the night,
Then returns the dark
With no more hope of light.

SECTION X

Sick, am I sick of a jealous dread?
Was not one of the two at her side
This new-made lord, whose splendor plucks
The slavish hat from the villager's head?
Whose old grandfather has lately died,
Gone to a blacker pit, for whom
Grimy nakedness dragging his trucks
And laying his trams in a poison'd gloom
Wrought, till he crept from a gutted mine
Master of half a servile shire,
And left his coal all turn'd into gold
To a grandson, first of his noble line,
Rich in the grace all women desire,
Strong in the power that all men adore,
And simper and set their voices lower,
And soften as if to a girl, and hold

Awe-stricken breaths at a work divine,
Seeing his gewgaw castle shine,
New as his title, built last year,
There amid perky larches and pine,
And over the sullen-purple moor—
Look at it—pricking a cockney ear.

What, has he found my jewel out?
For one of the two that rode at her side
Bound for the Hall, I am sure was he;
Bound for the Hall, and I think for a bride.
Blithe would her brother's acceptance be.
Maud could be gracious too, no doubt.
To a lord, a captain, a padded shape,
A bought commission, a waxen face,
A rabbit mouth that is ever agape—
Bought? what is it he cannot buy?
And therefore splenetic, personal, base,
A wounded thing with a rancorous cry,
At war with myself and a wretched race,
Sick, sick to the heart of life, am I.

Last week came one to the county town,
To preach our poor little army down,
And play the game of the despot kings,
Tho' the state has done it and thrice as well.
This broad-brimm'd hawker of holy things,
Whose ear is cramm'd with his cotton, and rings
Even in dreams to the chink of his pence,
This huckster put down war! can he tell
Whether war be a cause or a consequence?
Put down the passions that make earth hell!
Down with ambition, avarice, pride,

Jealousy, down! cut off from the mind
The bitter springs of anger and fear
Down too, down at your own fireside,
With the evil tongue and the evil ear,
For each is at war with mankind!

I wish I could hear again
The chivalrous battle-song
That she warbled alone in her joy!
I might persuade myself then
She would not do herself this great wrong,
To take a wanton dissolute boy
For a man and leader of men.

Ah God, for a man with heart, head, hand,
Like some of the simple great ones gone
For ever and ever by,
One still strong man in a blatant land,
Whatever they call him—what care I?—
Aristocrat, democrat, autocrat—one
Who can rule and dare not lie!

And ah for a man to arise in me,
That the man I am may cease to be!

Section XI

O, let the solid ground
    Not fail beneath my feet
Before my life has found
    What some have found so sweet!
Then let come what come may,
What matter if I go mad,
I shall have had my day.

Let the sweet heavens endure,
　Not close and darken above me
Before I am quite quite sure
　That there is one to love me!
Then let come what come may
To a life that has been so sad,
I shall have had my day.

Section XII

Birds in the high Hall-garden
　When twilight was falling,
Maud, Maud, Maud, Maud,
　They were crying and calling.

Where was Maud? in our wood;
　And I—who else?—was with her,
Gathering woodland lilies,
　Myriads blow together.

Birds in our wood sang
　Ringing thro' the valleys,
Maud is here, here, here
　In among the lilies.

I kiss'd her slender hand,
　She took the kiss sedately;
Maud is not seventeen,
　But she is tall and stately.

I to cry out on pride
　Who have won her favor!
O, Maud were sure of heaven
　If lowliness could save her!

I know the way she went
　　Home with her maiden posy,
For her feet have touch'd the meadows
　　And left the daisies rosy.

Birds in the high Hall-garden
　　Were crying and calling to her,
Where is Maud, Maud, Maud?
　　One is come to woo her.

Look, a horse at the door,
　　And little King Charley snarling!
Go back, my lord, across the moor,
　　You are not her darling.

Section XIII

Scorn'd, to be scorn'd by one that I scorn,
Is that a matter to make me fret?
That a calamity hard to be borne?
Well, he may live to hate me yet.
Fool that I am to be vext with his pride!
I past him, I was crossing his lands;
He stood on the path a little aside;
His face, as I grant, in spite of spite,
Has a broad-blown comeliness, red and white,
And six feet two, as I think, he stands;
But his essences turn'd the live air sick,
And barbarous opulence jewel-thick
Sunn'd itself on his breast and his hands.

Who shall call me ungentle, unfair?
I long'd so heartily then and there

To give him the grasp of fellowship
But while I past he was humming an air,
Stopt, and then with a riding-whip
Leisurely tapping a glossy boot
And curving a contumelious lip,
Gorgonized me from head to foot
With a stony British stare.

Why sits he here in his father's chair?
That old man never comes to his place;
Shall I believe him ashamed to be seen?
For only once, in the village street,
Last year, I caught a glimpse of his face,
A gray old wolf and a lean.
Scarcely, now, would I call him a cheat;
For then, perhaps, as a child of deceit,
She might by a true descent be untrue;
And Maud is as true as Maud is sweet,
Tho' I fancy her sweetness only due
To the sweeter blood by the other side;
Her mother has been a thing complete,
However she came to be so allied.
And fair without, faithful within,
Maud to him is nothing akin.
Some peculiar mystic grace
Made her only the child of her mother,
And heap'd the whole inherited sin
On that huge scapegoat of the race,
All, all upon the brother.

Peace, angry spirit, and let him be!
Has not his sister smiled on me?

Section XIV

Maud has a garden of roses
And lilies fair on a lawn;
There she walks in her state
And tends upon bed and bower,
And thither I climb'd at dawn
And stood by her garden-gate.
A lion ramps at the top,
He is claspt by a passion-flower.

Maud's own little oak-room—
Which Maud, like a precious stone
Set in the heart of the carven gloom
Lights with herself, when alone
She sits by her music and books
And her brother lingers late
With a roystering company—looks
Upon Maud's own garden-gate;
And I thought as I stood, if a hand, as white
As ocean-foam in the moon, were laid
On the hasp of the window, and my Delight
Had a sudden desire, like a glorious ghost, to glide,
Like a beam of the seventh heaven, down to my side,
There were but a step to be made.

The fancy flatter'd my mind,
And again seem'd overbold;
Now I thought that she cared for me,
Now I thought she was kind
Only because she was cold.

I heard no sound where I stood
But the rivulet on from the lawn

Running down to my own dark wood,
Or the voice of the long sea-wave as it swell'd
Now and then in the dim-gray dawn;
But I look'd, and round, all round the house I beheld
The death-white curtain drawn,
Felt a horror over me creep,
Prickle my skin and catch my breath
Knew that the death-white curtain meant but sleep,
Yet I shudder'd and thought like a fool of the sleep of death.

SECTION XV

So dark a mind within me dwells,
    And I make myself such evil cheer,
That if *I* be dear to some one else,
    Then some one else may have much to fear;
But if *I* be dear to some one else,
    Then I should be to myself more dear.
Shall I not take care of all that I think,
Yea, even of wretched meat and drink,
If I be dear,
If I be dear to some one else?

SECTION XVI

This lump of earth has left his estate
The lighter by the loss of his weight;
And so that he find what he went to seek,
And fulsome pleasure clog him, and drown
His heart in the gross mud-honey of town,
He may stay for a year who has gone for a week.
But this is the day when I must speak,
And I see my Oread coming down,
O, this is the day!

O beautiful creature, what am I
That I dare to look her way?
Think I may hold dominion sweet,
Lord of the pulse that is lord of her breast,
And dream of her beauty with tender dread,
From the delicate Arab arch of her feet
To the grace that, bright and light as the crest
Of a peacock, sits on her shining head,
And she knows it not—O, if she knew it,
To know her beauty might half undo it!
I know it the one bright thing to save
My yet young life in the wilds of Time,
Perhaps from madness, perhaps from crime,
Perhaps from a selfish grave.

What, if she be fasten'd to this fool lord,
Dare I bid her abide by her word?
Should I love her so well if she
Had given her word to a thing so low?
Shall I love her as well if she
Can break her word were it even for me?
I trust that it is not so.

Catch not my breath, O clamorous heart,
Let not my tongue be a thrall to my eye.
For I must tell her before we part,
I must tell her, or die.

SECTION XVII

Go not, happy day,
    From the shining fields,
Go not, happy day,
    Till the maiden yields,

Rosy is the West,
　Rosy is the South,
Roses are her cheeks,
　And a rose her mouth.
When the happy Yes
　Falters from her lips,
Pass and blush the news
　Over glowing ships;
Over blowing seas,
　Over seas at rest,
Pass the happy news,
　Blush it thro' the West;
Till the red man dance
　By his red cedar-tree,
And the red man's babe
　Leap, beyond the sea.
Blush from West to East,
　Blush from East to West,
Till the West is East,
　Blush it thro' the West.
Rosy is the West,
　Rosy is the South,
Roses are her cheeks,
　And a rose her mouth.

Section XVIII

I have led her home, my love, my only friend.
There is none like her, none.
And never yet so warmly ran my blood
And sweetly, on and on
Calming itself to the long-wish'd-for end,
Full to the banks, close on the promised good.

None like her, none.
Just now the dry-tongued laurels' pattering talk
Seem'd her light foot along the garden walk,
And shook my heart to think she comes once more.
But even then I heard her close the door;
The gates of heaven are closed, and she is gone.

There is none like her, none,
Nor will be when our summers have deceased.
O, art thou sighing for Lebanon
In the long breeze that streams to thy delicious East,
Sighing for Lebanon,
Dark cedar, tho' thy limbs have here increased,
Upon a pastoral slope as fair,
And looking to the South and fed
With honey'd rain and delicate air,
And haunted by the starry head
Of her whose gentle will has changed my fate,
And made my life a perfumed altar-flame;
And over whom thy darkness must have spread
With such delight as theirs of old, thy great
Forefathers of the thornless garden, there
Shadowing the snow-limb'd Eve from whom she came?

Here will I lie, while these long branches sway,
And you fair stars that crown a happy day
Go in and out as if at merry play,
Who am no more so all forlorn
As when it seem'd far better to be born
To labor and the mattock-harden'd hand
Than nursed at ease and brought to understand
A sad astrology, the boundless plan
That makes you tyrants in your iron skies,
Innumerable, pitiless, passionless eyes,

Cold fires, yet with power to burn and brand
His nothingness into man.

But now shine on, and what care I,
Who in this stormy gulf have found a pearl
The countercharm of space and hollow sky,
And do accept my madness, and would die
To save from some slight shame one simple girl?—

Would die, for sullen-seeming Death may give
More life to Love than is or ever was
In our low world, where yet 't is sweet to live.
Let no one ask me how it came to pass;
It seems that I am happy, that to me
A livelier emerald twinkles in the grass,
A purer sapphire melts into the sea.

Not die, but live a life of truest breath,
And teach true life to fight with mortal wrongs.
O, why should Love, like men in drinking-songs,
Spice his fair banquet with the dust of death?
Make answer, Maud my bliss,
Maud made my Maud by that long loving kiss,
Life of my life, wilt thou not answer this?
'The dusky strand of Death inwoven here
With dear Love's tie, makes Love himself more dear.'

Is that enchanted moan only the swell
Of the long waves that roll in yonder bay?
And hark the clock within, the silver knell
Of twelve sweet hours that past in bridal white,
And died to live, long as my pulses play;
But now by this my love has closed her sight
And given false death her hand, and stolen away

To dreamful wastes where footless fancies dwell
Among the fragments of the golden day.
May nothing there her maiden grace affright!
Dear heart, I feel with thee the drowsy spell.
My bride to be, my evermore delight,
My own heart's heart, my ownest own, farewell;
It is but for a little space I go.
And ye meanwhile far over moor and fell
Beat to the noiseless music of the night!
Has our whole earth gone nearer to the glow
Of your soft splendors that you look so bright?
I have climb'd nearer out of lonely hell.
Beat, happy stars, timing with things below,
Beat with my heart more blest than heart can tell,
Blest, but for some dark undercurrent woe
That seems to draw—but it shall not be so;
Let all be well, be well.

Section XIX

Her brother is coming back to-night,
Breaking up my dream of delight.

My dream? do I dream of bliss?
I have walk'd awake with Truth.
O, when did a morning shine
So rich in atonement as this
For my dark-dawning youth,
Darken'd watching a mother decline
And that dead man at her heart and mine;
For who was left to watch her but I?
Yet so did I let my freshness die.

I trust that I did not talk
To gentle Maud in our walk—
For often in lonely wanderings
I have cursed him even to lifeless things—
But I trust that I did not talk,
Not touch on her father's sin.
I am sure I did but speak
Of my mother's faded cheek
When it slowly grew so thin
That I felt she was slowly dying
Vext with lawyers and harass'd with debt;
For how often I caught her with eyes all wet,
Shaking her head at her son and sighing
A world of trouble within!

And Maud too, Maud was moved
To speak of the mother she loved
As one scarce less forlorn,
Dying abroad and it seems apart
From him who had ceased to share her heart,
And ever mourning over the feud,
The household Fury sprinkled with blood
By which our houses are torn.
How strange was what she said,
When only Maud and the brother
Hung over her dying bed—
That Maud's dark father and mine
Had bound us one to the other,
Betrothed us over their wine,
On the day when Maud was born;
Seal'd her mine from her first sweet breath!
Mine, mine by a right, from birth till death!
Mine, mine—our fathers have sworn!

But the true blood spilt had in it a heat
To dissolve the precious seal on a bond,
That, if left uncancell'd, had been so sweet;
And none of us thought of a something beyond,
A desire that awoke in the heart of the child,
As it were a duty done to the tomb,
To be friends for her sake, to be reconciled;
And I was cursing them and my doom,
And letting a dangerous thought run wild
While often abroad in the fragrant gloom
Of foreign churches—I see her there,
Bright English lily, breathing a prayer
To be friends, to be reconciled!

But then what a flint is he!
Abroad, at Florence, at Rome,
I find whenever she touch'd on me
This brother had laugh'd her down,
And at last, when each came home,
He had darken'd into a frown,
Chid her, and forbid her to speak
To me, her friend of the years before;
And this was what had redden'd her cheek
When I bow'd to her on the moor.

Yet Maud, altho' not blind
To the faults of his heart and mind,
I see she cannot but love him,
And says he is rough but kind,
And wishes me to approve him,
And tells me, when she lay
Sick once, with a fear of worse,

That he left his wine and horses and play,
Sat with her, read to her, night and day,
And tended her like a nurse.

Kind? but the death-bed desire
Spurn'd by this heir of the liar—
Rough but kind? yet I know
He has plotted against me in this,
That he plots against me still.
Kind to Maud? that were not amiss.
Well, rough but kind; why, let it be so,
For shall not Maud have her will?
For, Maud, so tender and true,
As long as my life endures
I feel I shall owe you a debt
That I never can hope to pay;
And if ever I should forget
That I owe this debt to you
And for your sweet sake to yours,
O, then, what then shall I say?—
If ever I *should* forget,
May God make me more wretched
Than ever I have been yet!

So now I have sworn to bury
All this dead body of hate,
I feel so free and so clear
By the loss of that dead weight,
That I should grow light-headed, I fear,
Fantastically merry,
But that her brother comes, like a blight
On my fresh hope, to the Hall to-night.

Section XX

Strange, that I felt so gay,
Strange, that *I* tried to-day
To beguile her melancholy;
The Sultan, as we name him—
She did not wish to blame him—
But he vext her and perplext her
With his worldly talk and folly.
Was it gentle to reprove her
For stealing out of view
From a little lazy lover
Who but claims her as his due?
Or for chilling his caresses
By the coldness of her manners,
Nay, the plainness of her dresses?
Now I know her but in two,
Nor can pronounce upon it
If one should ask me whether
The habit, hat, and feather,
Or the frock and gipsy bonnet
Be the neater and completer;
For nothing can be sweeter
Than maiden Maud in either.

But to-morrow, if we live,
Our ponderous squire will give
A grand political dinner
To half the squirelings near;
And Maud will wear her jewels,
And the bird of prey will hover,
And the titmouse hope to win her
With his chirrup at her ear.

A grand political dinner
To the men of many acres,
A gathering of the Tory,
A dinner and then a dance
For the maids and marriage-makers,
And every eye but mine will glance
At Maud in all her glory.

For I am not invited,
But, with the Sultan's pardon,
I am all as well delighted,
For I know her own rose-garden,
And mean to linger in it
Till the dancing will be over;
And then, O, then, come out to me
For a minute, but for a minute,
Come out to your own true lover,
That your true lover may see
Your glory also, and render
All homage to his own darling,
Queen Maud in all her splendor.

Section XXI

Rivulet crossing my ground,
And bringing me down from the Hall
This garden-rose that I found,
Forgetful of Maud and me,
And lost in trouble and moving round
Here at the head of a tinkling fall,
And trying to pass to the sea;
O rivulet, born at the Hall,
My Maud has sent it by thee—
If I read her sweet will right—

On a blushing mission to me,
Saying in odor and color, 'Ah, be
Among the roses to-night.'

Section XXII

Come into the garden, Maud,
  For the black bat, night, has flown,
Come into the garden, Maud,
  I am here at the gate alone;
And the woodbine spices are wafted abroad,
  And the musk of the rose is blown.

For a breeze of morning moves,
  And the planet of Love is on high,
Beginning to faint in the light that she loves
  On a bed of daffodil sky,
To faint in the light of the sun she loves,
  To faint in his light, and to die.

All night have the roses heard
  The flute, violin, bassoon;
All night has the casement jessamine stirr'd
  To the dancers dancing in tune;
Till a silence fell with the waking bird,
  And a hush with the setting moon.

I said to the lily, 'There is but one,
  With whom she has heart to be gay.
When will the dancers leave her alone?
  She is weary of dance and play.'
Now half to the setting moon are gone,
  And half to the rising day;
Low on the sand and loud on the stone
  The last wheel echoes away.

I said to the rose, 'The brief night goes
    In babble and revel and wine.
O young lord-lover, what sighs are those,
    For one that will never be thine?
But mine, but mine,' so I sware to the rose,
    'For ever and ever, mine.'

And the soul of the rose went into my blood,
    As the music clash'd in the hall;
And long by the garden lake I stood,
    For I heard your rivulet fall
From the lake to the meadow and on to the wood,
    Our wood, that is dearer than all;

From the meadow your walks have left so sweet
    That whenever a March-wind sighs
He sets the jewel-print of your feet
    In violets blue as your eyes,
To the woody hollows in which we meet
    And the valleys of Paradise.

The slender acacia would not shake
    One long milk-bloom on the tree;
The white lake-blossom fell into the lake
    As the pimpernel dozed on the lea;
But the rose was awake all night for your sake,
    Knowing your promise to me;
The lilies and roses were all awake,
    They sigh'd for the dawn and thee.

Queen rose of the rosebud garden of girls,
    Come hither, the dances are done,
In gloss of satin and glimmer of pearls,
    Queen lily and rose in one;

Shine out, little head, sunning over with curls,
  To the flowers, and be their sun.

There has fallen a splendid tear
  From the passion-flower at the gate.
She is coming, my dove, my dear;
  She is coming, my life, my fate.
The red rose cries, 'She is near, she is near;'
  And the white rose weeps, 'She is late;'
The larkspur listens, 'I hear, I hear;'
  And the lily whispers, 'I wait.'

She is coming, my own, my sweet;
  Were it ever so airy a tread,
My heart would hear her and beat,
  Were it earth in an earthy bed;
My dust would hear her and beat,
  Had I lain for a century dead,
Would start and tremble under her feet,
  And blossom in purple and red.

Part II

SECTION I

'The fault was mine, the fault was mine'—
Why am I sitting here so stunn'd and still,
Plucking the harmless wild-flower on the hill?—
It is this guilty hand!—
And there rises ever a passionate cry
From underneath in the darkening land—
What is it, that has been done?
O dawn of Eden bright over earth and sky,

The fires of hell brake out of thy rising sun,
The fires of hell and of hate;
For she, sweet soul, had hardly spoken a word,
When her brother ran in his rage to the gate,
He came with the babe-faced lord,
Heap'd on her terms of disgrace;
And while she wept, and I strove to be cool,
He fiercely gave me the lie,
Till I with as fierce an anger spoke,
And he struck me, madman, over the face,
Struck me before the languid fool,
Who was gaping and grinning by;
Struck for himself an evil stroke,
Wrought for his house an irredeemable woe.
For front to front in an hour we stood,
And a million horrible bellowing echoes broke
From the red-ribb'd hollow behind the wood,
And thunder'd up into heaven the Christless code
That must have life for a blow.
Ever and ever afresh they seem'd to grow.
Was it he lay there with a fading eye,
'The fault was mine,' he whisper'd, 'fly!'
Then glided out of the joyous wood
The ghastly Wraith of one that I know,
And there rang on a sudden a passionate cry,
A cry for a brother's blood;
It will ring in my heart and my ears till I die, till I die.

Is it gone? my pulses beat—
What was it? a lying trick of the brain?
Yet I thought I saw her stand,
A shadow there at my feet,
High over the shadowy land.
It is gone; and the heavens fall in a gentle rain,

When they should burst and drown with deluging
    storms
The feeble vassals of wine and anger and lust,
The little hearts that know not how to forgive.
Arise, my God, and strike, for we hold Thee just,
Strike dead the whole weak race of venomous worms,
That sting each other here in the dust;
We are not worthy to live.

Section II

See what a lovely shell,
Small and pure as a pearl,
Lying close to my foot,
Frail, but a work divine,
Made so fairily well
With delicate spire and whorl,
How exquisitely minute,
A miracle of design!

What is it? a learned man
Could give it a clumsy name.
Let him name it who can,
The beauty would be the same.

The tiny cell is forlorn,
Void of the little living will
That made it stir on the shore.
Did he stand at the diamond door
Of his house in a rainbow frill?
Did he push, when he was uncurl'd,
A golden foot or a fairy horn
Thro' his dim water-world?

Slight, to be crush'd with a tap
Of my finger-nail on the sand,
Small, but a work divine,
Frail, but of force to withstand,
Year upon year, the shock
Of cataract seas that snap
The three-decker's oaken spine
Athwart the ledges of rock,
Here on the Breton strand!

Breton, not Briton; here
Like a shipwreck'd man on a coast
Of ancient fable and fear—
Plagued with a flitting to and fro,
A disease, a hard mechanic ghost
That never came from on high
Nor ever arose from below,
But only moves with the moving eye,
Flying along the land and the main—
Why should it look like Maud?
Am I to be overawed
By what I cannot but know
Is a juggle born of the brain?

Back from the Breton coast,
Sick of a nameless fear,
Back to the dark sea-line
Looking, thinking of all I have lost;
An old song vexes my ear,
But that of Lamech is mine.

For years, a measureless ill,
For years, for ever, to part—
But she, she would love me still;

And as long, O God, as she
Have a grain of love for me,
So long, no doubt, no doubt,
Shall I nurse in my dark heart,
However weary, a spark of will
Not to be trampled out.

Strange, that the mind, when fraught
With a passion so intense
One would think that it well
Might drown all life in the eye,—
That it should, by being so over-wrought,
Suddenly strike on a sharper sense
For a shell, or a flower, little things
Which else would have been past by!
And now I remember, I,
When he lay dying there,
I noticed one of his many rings—
For he had many, poor worm—and thought,
It is his mother's hair.

Who knows if he be dead?
Whether I need have fled?
Am I guilty of blood?
However this may be,
Comfort her, comfort her, all things good,
While I am over the sea!
Let me and my passionate love go by,
But speak to her all things holy and high,
Whatever happen to me!
Me and my harmful love go by;
But come to her waking, find her asleep,
Powers of the height, Powers of the deep,
And comfort her tho' I die!

Section III

Courage, poor heart of stone!
I will not ask thee why
Thou canst not understand
That thou art left for ever alone;
Courage, poor stupid heart of stone!—
Or if I ask thee why,
Care not thou to reply:
She is but dead, and the time is at hand
When thou shalt more than die.

Section IV

O that 't were possible
After long grief and pain
To find the arms of my true love
Round me once again!

When I was wont to meet her
In the silent woody places
By the home that gave me birth,
We stood tranced in long embraces
Mixt with kisses sweeter, sweeter
Than anything on earth.

A shadow flits before me,
Not thou, but like to thee.
Ah, Christ, that it were possible
For one short hour to see
The souls we loved, that they might tell us
What and where they be!

It leads me forth at evening,
It lightly winds and steals
In a cold white robe before me,
When all my spirit reels
At the shouts, the leagues of lights,
And the roaring of the wheels.

Half the night I waste in sighs,
Half in dreams I sorrow after
The delight of early skies;
In a wakeful doze I sorrow
For the hand, the lips, the eyes,
For the meeting of the morrow,
The delight of happy laughter,
The delight of low replies.

'T is a morning pure and sweet,
And a dewy splendor falls
On the little flower that clings
To the turrets and the walls;
'T is a morning pure and sweet,
And the light and shadow fleet.
She is walking in the meadow,
And the woodland echo rings;
In a moment we shall meet.
She is singing in the meadow,
And the rivulet at her feet
Ripples on in light and shadow
To the ballad that she sings.

Do I hear her sing as of old,
My bird with the shining head,
My own dove with the tender eye?

But there rings on a sudden a passionate cry,
There is some one dying or dead,
And a sullen thunder is roll'd;
For a tumult shakes the city,
And I wake, my dream is fled.
In the shuddering dawn, behold,
Without knowledge, without pity,
By the curtains of my bed
That abiding phantom cold!

Get thee hence, nor come again,
Mix not memory with doubt,
Pass, thou deathlike type of pain,
Pass and cease to move about!
'T is the blot upon the brain
That *will* show itself without.

Then I rise, the eave-drops fall,
And the yellow vapors choke
The great city sounding wide;
The day comes, a dull red ball
Wrapt in drifts of lurid smoke
On the misty river-tide.

Thro' the hubbub of the market
I steal, a wasted frame;
It crosses here, it crosses there,
Thro' all that crowd confused and loud,
The shadow still the same;
And on my heavy eyelids
My anguish hangs like shame.

Alas for her that met me,
That heard me softly call,

Came glimmering thro' the laurels
At the quiet evenfall,
In the garden by the turrets
Of the old manorial hall!

Would the happy spirit descend
From the realms of light and song,
In the chamber or the street,
As she looks among the blest,
Should I fear to greet my friend
Or to say, 'Forgive the wrong,'
Or to ask her, 'Take me, sweet,
To the regions of thy rest'?

But the broad light glares and beats,
And the shadow flits and fleets
And will not let me be;
And I loathe the squares and streets,
And the faces that one meets,
Hearts with no love for me.
Always I long to creep
Into some still cavern deep,
There to weep, and weep, and weep
My whole soul out to thee.

Section V

Dead, long dead,
Long dead!
And my heart is a handful of dust,
And the wheels go over my head,
And my bones are shaken with pain,
For into a shallow grave they are thrust,
Only a yard beneath the street,

And the hoofs of the horses beat, beat,
The hoofs of the horses beat,
Beat into my scalp and my brain,
With never an end to the stream of passing feet,
Driving, hurrying, marrying, burying,
Clamor and rumble, and ringing and clatter;
And here beneath it is all as bad,
For I thought the dead had peace, but it is not so.
To have no peace in the grave, is that not sad?
But up and down and to and fro,
Ever about me the dead men go;
And then to hear a dead man chatter
Is enough to drive one mad.

Wretchedest age, since Time began,
They cannot even bury a man;
And tho' we paid our tithes in the days that are gone,
Not a bell was rung, not a prayer was read.
It is that which makes us loud in the world of the dead;
There is none that does his work, not one.
A touch of their office might have sufficed,
But the churchmen fain would kill their church,
As the churches have kill'd their Christ.

See, there is one of us sobbing,
No limit to his distress;
And another, a lord of all things, praying
To his own great self, as I guess;
And another, a statesman there, betraying
His party-secret, fool, to the press;
And yonder a vile physician, blabbing
The case of his patient—all for what?
To tickle the maggot born in an empty head,

And wheedle a world that loves him not,
For it is but a world of the dead.

Nothing but idiot gabble!
For the prophecy given of old
And then not understood,
Has come to pass as foretold;
Not let any man think for the public good,
But babble, merely for babble.
For I never whisper'd a private affair
Within the hearing of cat or mouse,
No, not to myself in the closet alone,
But I heard it shouted at once from the top of the house;
Everything came to be known.
Who told *him* we were there?

Not that gray old wolf, for he came not back
From the wilderness, full of wolves, where he used to lie;
He has gather'd the bones for his o'ergrown whelp to crack—
Crack them now for yourself, and howl, and die.

Prophet, curse me the blabbing lip,
And curse me the British vermin, the rat;
I know not whether he came in the Hanover ship,
But I know that he lies and listens mute
In an ancient mansion's crannies and holes.
Arsenic, arsenic, sure, would do it,
Except that now we poison our babes, poor souls!
It is all used up for that.

Tell him now: she is standing here at my head;
Not beautiful now, not even kind;
He may take her now; for she never speaks her mind,
But is ever the one thing silent here.

She is not *of* us, as I divine;
She comes from another stiller world of the dead,
Stiller, not fairer than mine.

But I know where a garden grows,
Fairer than aught in the world beside,
All made up of the lily and rose
That blow by night, when the season is good,
To the sound of dancing music and flutes:
It is only flowers, they had no fruits,
And I almost fear they are not roses, but blood;
For the keeper was one, so full of pride,
He linkt a dead man there to a spectral bride;
For he, if he had not been a Sultan of brutes,
Would he have that hole in his side?

But what will the old man say?
He laid a cruel snare in a pit
To catch a friend of mine one stormy day;
Yet now I could even weep to think of it;
For what will the old man say
When he comes to the second corpse in the pit?

Friend, to be struck by the public foe,
Then to strike him and lay him low,
That were a public merit, far,
Whatever the Quaker holds, from sin;
But the red life spilt for a private blow—
I swear to you, lawful and lawless war
Are scarcely even akin.

O me, why have they not buried me deep enough?
Is it kind to have made me a grave so rough,
Me, that was never a quiet sleeper?

Maybe still I am but half-dead;
Then I cannot be wholly dumb.
I will cry to the steps above my head
And somebody, surely, some kind heart will come
To bury me, bury me
Deeper, ever so little deeper.

Part III

My life has crept so long on a broken wing
Thro' cells of madness, haunts of horror and fear,
That I come to be grateful at last for a little thing
My mood is changed, for it fell at a time of year
When the face of night is fair on the dewy downs,
And the shining daffodil dies, and the Charioteer
And starry Gemini hang like glorious crowns
Over Orion's grave low down in the west,
That like a silent lightning under the stars
She seem'd to divide in a dream from a band of the blest,
And spoke of a hope for the world in the coming wars—
'And in that hope, dear soul, let trouble have rest,
Knowing I tarry for thee,' and pointed to Mars
As he glow'd like a ruddy shield on the Lion's breast.

And it was but a dream, yet it yielded a dear delight
To have look'd, tho' but in a dream upon eyes so fair,
That had been in a weary world my one thing bright;
And it was but a dream, yet it lighten'd my despair
When I thought that a war would arise in defence of the
    right,
That an iron tyranny now should bend or cease,
The glory of manhood stand on his ancient height,
Nor Britain's one sole God be the millionaire.

No more shall commerce be all in all, and Peace
Pipe on her pastoral hillock a languid note,
And watch her harvest ripen, her herd increase,
Nor the cannon-bullet rust on a slothful shore,
And the cobweb woven across the cannon's throat
Shall shake its threaded tears in the wind no more.

And as months ran on and rumor of battle grew,
'It is time, it is time, O passionate heart,' said I,—
For I cleaved to a cause that I felt to be pure and true,—
'It is time, O passionate heart and morbid eye,
That old hysterical mock-disease should die,'
And I stood on a giant deck and mixt my breath
With a loyal people shouting a battle-cry,
Till I saw the dreary phantom arise and fly
Far into the North, and battle, and seas of death.

Let it go or stay, so I wake to the higher aims
Of a land that has lost for a little her lust of gold,
And love of a peace that was full of wrongs and shames,
Horrible, hateful, monstrous, not to be told;
And hail once more to the banner of battle unroll'd!
Tho' many a light shall darken, and many shall weep
For those that are crush'd in the clash of jarring claims,
Yet God's just wrath shall be wreak'd on a giant liar,
And many a darkness into the light shall leap,
And shine in the sudden making of splendid names,
And noble thought be freer under the sun,
And the heart of a people beat with one desire;
For the peace, that I deem'd no peace, is over and done,
And now by the side of the Black and the Baltic deep,
And deathful-grinning mouths of the fortress, flames
The blood-red blossom of war with a heart of fire.

Let it flame or fade, and the war roll down like a wind,
We have proved we have hearts in a cause, we are noble still,
And myself have awaked, as it seems, to the better mind.
It is better to fight for the good than to rail at the ill;
I have felt with my native land, I am one with my kind,
I embrace the purpose of God, and the doom assign'd.

———

LOCKSLEY HALL

COMRADES, leave me here a little, while as yet 't is early
    morn;
Leave me here, and when you want me, sound upon the
    bugle-horn.

'T is the place, and all around it, as of old, the curlews call,
Dreary gleams about the moorland flying over Locksley Hall;

Locksley Hall, that in the distance overlooks the sandy tracts,
And the hollow ocean-ridges roaring into cataracts.

Many a night from yonder ivied casement, ere I went to rest,
Did I look on great Orion sloping slowly to the west.

Many a night I saw the Pleiads, rising thro' the mellow shade,
Glitter like a swarm of fireflies tangled in a silver braid.

Here about the beach I wander'd, nourishing a youth sublime
With the fairy tales of science, and the long result of time;

When the centuries behind me like a fruitful land reposed;
When I clung to all the present for the promise that it closed;

When I dipt into the future far as human eye could see,
Saw the vision of the world and all the wonder that would
  be.—

In the spring a fuller crimson comes upon the robin's breast;
In the spring the wanton lapwing gets himself another crest;

In the spring a livelier iris changes on the burnish'd dove;
In the spring a young man's fancy lightly turns to thoughts
  of love.

Then her cheek was pale and thinner than should be for one
  so young,
And her eyes on all my motions with a mute observance hung.

And I said, 'My cousin Amy, speak, and speak the truth to
  me,
Trust me, cousin, all the current of my being sets to thee.'

On her pallid cheek and forehead came a color and a light,
As I have seen the rosy red flushing in the northern night.

And she turn'd—her bosom shaken with a sudden storm of
  sighs—
All the spirit deeply dawning in the dark of hazel eyes—

Saying, 'I have hid my feelings, fearing they should do me
  wrong;'
Saying, 'Dost thou love me, cousin?' weeping, 'I have loved
  thee long.'

Love took up the glass of Time, and turn'd it in his glowing
  hands;
Every moment, lightly shaken, ran itself in golden sands.

Love took up the harp of Life, and smote on all the chords
  with might;
Smote the chord of Self, that, trembling, past in music out
  of sight.

Many a morning on the moorland did we hear the copses ring,
And her whisper throng'd my pulses with the fulness of the
  spring.

Many an evening by the waters did we watch the stately
  ships,
And our spirits rush'd together at the touching of the lips.

O my cousin, shallow-hearted!   O my Amy, mine no more!
O the dreary, dreary moorland!   O the barren, barren shore!

Falser than all fancy fathoms, falser than all songs have sung,
Puppet to a father's threat, and servile to a shrewish tongue!

Is it well to wish thee happy?—having known me—to decline
On a range of lower feelings and a narrower heart than mine!

Yet it shall be; thou shalt lower to his level day by day,
What is fine within thee growing coarse to sympathize with
  clay.

As the husband is, the wife is; thou art mated with a clown,
And the grossness of his nature will have weight to drag thee
  down.

He will hold thee, when his passion shall have spent its novel
  force,
Something better than his dog, a little dearer than his horse.

What is this? his eyes are heavy; think not they are glazed
with wine.
Go to him, it is thy duty; kiss him, take his hand in thine.

It may be my lord is weary, that his brain is overwrought;
Soothe him with thy finer fancies, touch him with thy lighter
thought.

He will answer to the purpose, easy things to understand—
Better thou wert dead before me tho' I slew thee with my
hand!

Better thou and I were lying, hidden from the heart's disgrace,
Roll'd in one another's arms, and silent in a last embrace.

Cursed be the social wants that sin against the strength of
youth!
Cursed be the social lies that warp us from the living truth!

Cursed be the sickly forms that err from honest Nature's
rule!
Cursed be the gold that gilds the straiten'd forehead of the
fool!

Well—'t is well that I should bluster!— Hadst thou less
unworthy proved—
Would to God—for I had loved thee more than ever wife was
loved.

Am I mad, that I should cherish that which bears but bitter
fruit?
I will pluck it from my bosom, tho' my heart be at the root.

Never, tho' my mortal summers to such length of years should
come
As the many-winter'd crow that leads the clanging rookery
home.

Where is comfort? in division of the records of the mind?
Can I part her from herself, and love her, as I knew her,
kind?

I remembered one that perish'd; sweetly did she speak and
move;
Such a one do I remember, whom to look at was to love.

Can I think of her as dead, and love her for the love she bore?
No—she never loved me truly; love is love for evermore.

Comfort? comfort scorn'd of devils! this is truth the poet
sings,
That a sorrow's crown of sorrow is remembering happier
things.

Drug thy memories, lest thou learn it, lest thy heart be put
to proof,
In the dead unhappy night, and when the rain is on the roof.

Like a dog, he hunts in dreams, and thou art staring at the wall,
Where the dying night-lamp flickers, and the shadows rise and
fall.

Then a hand shall pass before thee, pointing to his drunken
sleep,
To thy widow'd marriage-pillows, to the tears that thou wilt
weep.

Thou shalt hear the 'Never, never,' whisper'd by the phantom
years,
And a song from out the distance in the ringing of thine ears;

And an eye shall vex thee, looking ancient kindness on thy
pain.
Turn thee, turn thee on thy pillow, get thee to thy rest again.

Nay, but Nature brings thee solace; for a tender voice will
cry.
'T is a purer life than thine, a lip to drain thy trouble dry.

Baby lips will laugh me down; my latest rival brings thee rest.
Baby fingers, waxen touches, press me from the mother's
breast.

O, the child too clothes the father with a dearness not his due.
Half is thine and half is his; it will be worthy of the two.

O, I see thee old and formal, fitted to thy petty part,
With a little hoard of maxims preaching down a daughter's
heart.

'They were dangerous guides the feelings—she herself was not
exempt—
Truly, she herself had suffer'd'—Perish in thy self-contempt!

Overlive it—lower yet—be happy! wherefore should I care?
I myself must mix with action, lest I wither by despair.

What is that which I should turn to, lighting upon days like
these?
Every door is barr'd with gold, and opens but to golden keys.

Every gate is throng'd with suitors, all the markets overflow.
I have but an angry fancy; what is that which I should do?

I had been content to perish, falling on the foeman's ground,
When the ranks are roll'd in vapor, and the winds are laid
with sound.

But the jingling of the guinea helps the hurt that Honor
feels,
And the nations do but murmur, snarling at each other's heels.

Can I but relive in sadness? I will turn that earlier page.
Hide me from my deep emotion, O thou wondrous Mother-
Age!

Make me feel the wild pulsation that I felt before the strife,
When I heard my days before me, and the tumult of my life;

Yearning for the large excitement that the coming years
would yield,
Eager-hearted as a boy when first he leaves his father's field,

And at night along the dusky highway near and nearer drawn,
Sees in heaven the light of London flaring like a dreary dawn;

And his spirit leaps within him to be gone before him then,
Underneath the light he looks at, in among the throngs of
men;

Men, my brothers, men the workers, ever reaping something
new;
That which they have done but earnest of the things that
they shall do.

For I dipt into the future, far as human eye could see,
Saw the Vision of the world, and all the wonder that would
   be;

Saw the heavens fill with commerce, argosies of magic sails,
Pilots of the purple twilight, dropping down with costly bales;

Heard the heavens fill with shouting, and there rain'd a
   ghastly dew
From the nations' airy navies grappling in the central blue;

Far along the world-wide whisper of the south-wind rushing
   warm,
With the standards of the peoples plunging thro' the thunder-
   storm;

Till the war-drum throbb'd no longer, and the battle-flags
   were furl'd
In the Parliament of man, the Federation of the world.

There the common sense of most shall hold a fretful realm in
   awe,
And the kindly earth shall slumber, lapt in universal law.

So I triumph'd ere my passion sweeping thro' me left me dry,
Left me with the palsied heart, and left me with the jaundiced
   eye;

Eye, to which all order festers, all things here are out of joint.
Science moves, but slowly, slowly, creeping on from point to
   point;

Slowly comes a hungry people, as a lion, creeping nigher,
Glares at one that nods and winks behind a slowly-dying fire.

Yet I doubt not thro' the ages one increasing purpose runs,
And the thoughts of men are widen'd with the process of the
suns.

What is that to him that reaps not harvest of his youthful
joys,
Tho' the deep heart of existence beat for ever like a boy's?

Knowledge comes, but wisdom lingers, and I linger on the
shore,
And the individual withers, and the world is more and more.

Knowledge comes, but wisdom lingers, and he bears a laden
breast,
Full of sad experience, moving toward the stillness of his rest.

Hark, my merry comrades call me, sounding on the bugle-
horn,
They to whom my foolish passion were a target for their
scorn.

Shall it not be scorn to me to harp on such a moulder'd
string?
I am shamed thro' all my nature to have loved so slight a
thing.

Weakness to be wroth with weakness! woman's pleasure,
woman's pain—
Nature made them blinder motions bounded in a shallower
brain.

Woman is the lesser man, and all thy passions, match'd with
mine,
Are as moonlight unto sunlight, and as water unto wine—

Here at least, where nature sickens, nothing. Ah, for some
    retreat
Deep in yonder shining Orient, where my life began to beat,

Where in wild Mahratta-battle fell my father evil-starr'd;—
I was left a trampled orphan, and a selfish uncle's ward.

Or to burst all links of habit—there to wander far away,
On from island unto island at the gateways of the day.

Larger constellations burning, mellow moons and happy skies,
Breadths of tropic shade and palms in cluster, knots of
    Paradise.

Never comes the trader, never floats an European flag,
Slides the bird o'er lustrous woodland, swings the trailer from
    the crag;

Droops the heavy blossom'd bower, hangs the heavy-fruited
    tree—
Summer isles of Eden lying in dark-purple spheres of sea.

There methinks would be enjoyment more than in this march
    of mind,
In the steamship, in the railway, in the thoughts that shake
    mankind.

There the passions cramp'd no longer shall have scope and
    breathing space;
I will take some savage woman, she shall rear my dusky race.

Iron-jointed, supple-sinew'd, they shall dive, and they shall
    run,
Catch the wild goat by the hair, and hurl their lances in the
    sun;

Whistle back the parrot's call, and leap the rainbows of the
  brooks,
Not with blinded eyesight poring over miserable books—

Fool, again the dream, the fancy! but I *know* my words are
  wild,
But I count the gray barbarian lower than the Christian child.

I, to herd with narrow foreheads, vacant of our glorious gains,
Like a beast with lower pleasures, like a beast with lower
  pains!

Mated with a squalid savage—what to me were sun or clime?
I the heir of all the ages, in the foremost files of time—

I that rather held it better men should perish one by one,
Than that earth should stand at gaze like Joshua's moon in
  Ajalon!

Not in vain the distance beacons. Forward, forward let us
  range,
Let the great world spin for ever down the ringing grooves
  of change.

Thro' the shadow of the globe we sweep into the younger day;
Better fifty years of Europe than a cycle of Cathay.

Mother-Age,—for mine I knew not,—help me as when life
  begun;
Rift the hills, and roll the waters, flash the lightnings, weigh
  the sun.

O, I see the crescent promise of my spirit hath not set.
Ancient founts of inspiration well thro' all my fancy yet.

Howsoever these things be, a long farewell to Locksley Hall!
Now for me the woods may wither, now for me the roof-tree
fall.

Comes a vapor from the margin, blackening over heath and
holt,
Cramming all the blast before it, in its breast a thunderbolt.

Let it fall on Locksley Hall, with rain or hail, or fire or snow;
For the mighty wind arises, roaring seaward, and I go.

RIZPAH

17—

WAILING, wailing, wailing, the wind over land and sea—
And Willy's voice in the wind, 'O mother, come out to me!'
Why should he call me to-night, when he knows that I can-
not go?
For the downs are as bright as day, and the full moon stares
at the snow.

We should be seen, my dear; they would spy us out of the
town.
The loud black nights for us, and the storm rushing over the
down,
When I cannot see my own hand, but am led by the creak of
the chain,
And grovel and grope for my son till I find myself drenched
with the rain.

Anything fallen again? nay—what was there left to fall?
I have taken them home, I have number'd the bones, I have
hidden them all.

What am I saying? and what are *you?* do you come as a spy?
Falls? what falls? who knows? As the tree falls so must
   it lie.

Who let her in? how long has she been? you—what have you
   heard?
Why did you sit so quiet? you never have spoken a word.
O—to pray with me—yes—a lady—none of their spies—
But the night has crept into my heart, and begun to darken
   my eyes.

Ah—you, that have lived so soft, what should *you* know of
   the night,
The blast and the burning shame and the bitter frost and the
   fright?
I have done it, while you were asleep—you were only made
   for the day.
I have gather'd my baby together—and now you may go
   your way.

Nay—for it's kind of you, madam, to sit by an old dying wife.
But say nothing hard of my boy, I have only an hour of life.
I kiss'd my boy in the prison, before he went out to die.
'They dared me to do it,' he said, and he never has told me
   a lie.
I whipt him for robbing an orchard once when he was but a
   child—
'The farmer dared me to do it,' he said; he was always so
   wild—
And idle—and couldn't be idle—my Willy—he never could
   rest.
The King should have made him a soldier, he would have
   been one of his best

But he lived with a lot of wild mates, and they never would
    let him be good;
They swore that he dare not rob the mail, and he swore that
    he would;
And he took no life, but he took one purse, and when all was
    done
He flung it among his fellows—'I'll none of it,' said my son.

I came into court to the judge and the lawyers. I told them
    my tale,
God's own truth—but they kill'd him, they kill'd him for
    robbing the mail.
They hang'd him in chains for a show—we had always borne
    a good name—
To be hang'd for a thief—and then put away—isn't that
    enough shame?
Dust to dust—low down—let us hide! but they set him so
    high
That all the ships of the world could stare at him, passing by.
God 'ill pardon the hell-black raven and horrible fowls of the
    air,
But not the black heart of the lawyer who kill'd him and
    hang'd him there.

And the jailer forced me away. I had bid him my last good-
    bye;
They had fasten'd the door of his cell. 'O mother!' I heard
    him cry.
I couldn't get back tho' I tried, he had something further to
    say,
And now I never shall know it. The jailer forced me away.

Then since I couldn't but hear that cry of my boy that was
    dead,

They seized me and shut me up: they fasten'd me down on
my bed.

'Mother, O mother!'—he call'd in the dark to me year after
year—

They beat me for that, they beat me—you know that I
couldn't but hear;

And then at the last they found I had grown so stupid and
still

They let me abroad again—but the creatures had worked
their will.

Flesh of my flesh was gone, but bone of my bone was left—

I stole them all from the lawyers—and you, will you call it a
theft?—

My baby, the bones that had suck'd me, the bones that had
laughed and had cried—

Theirs? O, no! they are mine—not theirs—they had moved
in my side.

Do you think I was scared by the bones? I kiss'd 'em, I
buried 'em all—

I can't dig deep, I am old—in the night by the churchyard
wall.

My Willy 'll rise up whole when the trumpet of judgment
'ill sound,

But I charge you never to say that I laid him in holy ground.

They would scratch him up—they would hang him again on
the cursed tree.

Sin? O, yes, we are sinners, I know—let all that be,

And read me a Bible verse of the Lord's goodwill toward
men—

'Full of compassion and mercy, the Lord'—let me hear it
again;

'Full of compassion and mercy—long-suffering.' Yes, O yes!

For the lawyer is born but to murder—the Saviour lives but to bless.

He 'll never put on the black cap except for the worst of the worst,

And the first may be last—I have heard it in church—and the last may be first.

Suffering—O, long-suffering—yes, as the Lord must know,

Year after year in the mist and the wind and the shower and the snow.

Heard, have you? what? they have told you he never repented his sin.

How do they know it? are *they* his mother? are *you* of his kin?

Heard! have you ever heard, when the storm on the downs began,

The wind that 'ill wail like a child and the sea that 'ill moan like a man?

Election, Election, and Reprobation—it's all very well.

But I go to-night to my boy, and I shall not find him in hell.

For I cared so much for my boy that the Lord has look'd into my care,

And He means me I'm sure to be happy with Willy, I know not where.

And if *he* be lost—but to save *my* soul, that is all your desire—

Do you think that I care for *my* soul if my boy be gone to the fire?

I have been with God in the dark—go, go, you may leave me alone—

You never have borne a child—you are just as hard as a stone.

Madam, I beg your pardon! I think that you mean to be
  kind,
But I cannot hear what you say for my Willy's voice in the
  wind—
The snow and the sky so bright—he used but to call in the
  dark,
And he calls to me now from the church and not from the
  gibbet—for hark!
Nay—you can hear it yourself—it is coming—shaking the
  walls—
Willy—the moon's in a cloud—Good-night. I am going.
  He calls.

SONGS

THE PRINCESS

As THRO' the land at eve we went,
  And pluck'd the ripen'd ears,
We fell out, my wife and I,
O, we fell out, I know not why,
  And kiss'd again with tears.
And blessings on the falling out
  That all the more endears,
When we fall out with those we love
  And kiss again with tears!
For when we came where lies the child
  We lost in other years,
There above the little grave,
O, there above the little grave,
  We kiss'd again with tears.

  Sweet and low, sweet and low,
    Wind of the western sea,
  Low, low, breathe and blow,
    Wind of the western sea!
    Over the rolling waters go,
    Come from the dying moon, and blow,
      Blow him again to me;
While my little one, while my pretty one sleeps.

  Sleep and rest, sleep and rest,
    Father will come to thee soon;

Rest, rest, on mother's breast,
 Father will come to thee soon;
Father will come to his babe in the nest,
Silver sails all out of the west
 Under the silver moon;
Sleep, my little one, sleep, my pretty one, sleep.

The splendor falls on castle walls
 And snowy summits old in story;
The long light shakes across the lakes,
 And the wild cataract leaps in glory.
Blow, bugle, blow, set the wild echoes flying,
Blow, bugle; answer, echoes, dying, dying, dying.

O, hark, O, hear! how thin and clear,
 And thinner, clearer, farther going!
O, sweet and far from cliff and scar
 The horns of Elfland faintly blowing!
Blow, let us hear the purple glens replying,
Blow, bugle; answer, echoes, dying, dying, dying.

O love, they die in yon rich sky,
 They faint on hill or field or river;
Our echoes roll from soul to soul,
 And grow for ever and for ever.
Blow, bugle, blow, set the wild echoes flying,
And answer, echoes, answer, dying, dying, dying.

'Tears, idle tears, I know not what they mean,
Tears from the depth of some divine despair
Rise in the heart, and gather to the eyes,
In looking on the happy autumn-fields,
And thinking of the days that are no more.

'Fresh as the first beam glittering on a sail,
That brings our friends up from the underworld,
Sad as the last which reddens over one
That sinks with all we love below the verge;
So sad, so fresh, the days that are no more.

'Ah, sad and strange as in dark summer dawns
The earliest pipe of half-awaken'd birds
To dying ears, when unto dying eyes
The casement slowly grows a glimmering square;
So sad, so strange, the days that are no more.

'Dear as remember'd kisses after death,
And sweet as those by hopeless fancy feign'd
On lips that are for others; deep as love,
Deep as first love, and wild with all regret;
O Death in Life, the days that are no more!'

'O Swallow, Swallow, flying, flying south,
Fly to her, and fall upon her gilded eaves,
And tell her, tell her, what I tell to thee.

'O, tell her, Swallow, thou that knowest each,
That bright and fierce and fickle is the South,
And dark and true and tender is the North.

'O Swallow, Swallow, if I could follow, and light
Upon her lattice, I would pipe and trill,
And cheep and twitter twenty million loves.

'O, were I thou that she might take me in,
And lay me on her bosom, and her heart
Would rock the snowy cradle till I died!

'Why lingereth she to clothe her heart with love,
Delaying as the tender ash delays
To clothe herself, when all the woods are green?

'O, tell her, Swallow, that thy brood is flown;
Say to her, I do but wanton in the South,
But in the North long since my nest is made.

'O, tell her, brief is life but love is long,
And brief the sun of summer in the North,
And brief the moon of beauty in the South.

'O Swallow, flying from the golden woods,
Fly to her, and pipe and woo her, and make her mine,
And tell her, tell her that I follow thee.'

Thy voice is heard thro' rolling drums
    That beat to battle where he stands;
Thy face across his fancy comes,
    And gives the battle to his hands.
A moment, while the trumpets blow,
    He sees his brood about thy knee;
The next, like fire he meets the foe,
    And strikes him dead for thine and thee.

Home they brought her warrior dead;
    She nor swoon'd nor utter'd cry.
All her maidens, watching, said,
    'She must weep or she will die.'

Then they praised him, soft and low,
    Call'd him worthy to be loved,
Truest friend and noblest foe;
    Yet she neither spoke nor moved.

Stole a maiden from her place,
  Lightly to the warrior stept,
Took the face-cloth from the face;
  Yet she neither moved nor wept.

Rose a nurse of ninety years,
  Set his child upon her knee—
Like summer tempest came her tears—
  'Sweet my child, I live for thee.'

  'Our enemies have fallen, have fallen: the seed,
The little seed they laugh'd at in the dark,
Has risen and cleft the soil, and grown a bulk
Of spanless girth, that lays on every side
A thousand arms and rushes to the sun.

  'Our enemies have fallen, have fallen: they came;
The leaves were wet with women's tears; they heard
A noise of songs they would not understand;
They mark'd it with the red cross to the fall,
And would have strown it, and are fallen themselves.

  'Our enemies have fallen, have fallen: they came;
The woodmen with their axes: lo the tree!
But we will make it faggots for the hearth,
And shape it plank and beam for roof and floor,
And boats and bridges for the use of men.

  'Our enemies have fallen, have fallen; they struck;
With their own blows they hurt themselves, nor knew
There dwelt an iron nature in the grain;
The glittering axe was broken in their arms,
Their arms were shatter'd to the shoulder blade.

'Our enemies have fallen, but this shall grow
A night of Summer from the heat, a breadth
Of Autumn, dropping fruits of power; and roll'd
With music in the growing breeze of Time,
The tops shall strike from star to star, the fangs
Shall move the stony bases of the world.

Ask me no more: the moon may draw the sea;
  The cloud may stoop from heaven and take the shape,
  With fold to fold, of mountain or of cape;
But O too fond, when have I answer'd thee?
                Ask me no more.

Ask me no more: what answer should I give?
  I love not hollow cheek or faded eye:
  Yet, O my friend, I will not have thee die!
Ask me no more, lest I should bid thee live;
                Ask me no more.

Ask me no more: thy fate and mine are seal'd;
  I strove against the stream and all in vain;
  Let the great river take me to the main.
No more, dear love, for at a touch I yield;
                Ask me no more.

'Now sleeps the crimson petal, now the white;
Nor waves the cypress in the palace walk;
Nor winks the gold fin in the porphyry font.
The fire-fly wakens; waken thou with me.

'Now droops the milk-white peacock like a ghost,
And like a ghost she glimmers on to me.

'Now lies the Earth all Danaë to the stars,
And all thy heart lies open unto me.

'Now slides the silent meteor on, and leaves
A shining furrow, as thy thoughts in me.

'Now folds the lily all her sweetness up,
And slips into the bosom of the lake.
So fold thyself, my dearest, thou, and slip
Into my bosom and be lost in me.'

'Come down, O maid, from yonder mountain height.
What pleasure lives in height (the shepherd sang),
In height and cold, the splendor of the hills?
But cease to move so near the heavens, and cease
To glide a sunbeam by the blasted pine,
To sit a star upon the sparkling spire;
And come, for Love is of the valley, come,
For Love is of the valley, come thou down
And find him; by the happy threshold, he,
Or hand in hand with Plenty in the maize,
Or red with spirted purple of the vats,
Or foxlike in the vine; nor cares to walk
With Death and Morning on the Silver Horns,
Nor wilt thou snare him in the white ravine,
Nor find him dropt upon the firths of ice,
That huddling slant in furrow-cloven falls
To roll the torrent out of dusky doors.
But follow; let the torrent dance thee down
To find him in the valley; let the wild
Lean-headed eagles yelp alone, and leave
The monstrous ledges there to slope, and spill
Their thousand wreaths of dangling water-smoke,
That like a broken purpose waste in air.
So waste not thou, but come; for all the vales
Await thee; azure pillars of the hearth
Arise to thee; the children call, and I

Thy shepherd pipe, and sweet is every sound,
Sweeter thy voice, but every sound is sweet;
Myriads of rivulets hurrying thro' the lawn,
The moan of doves in immemorial elms,
And murmuring of innumerable bees.'

THE BROOK

I COME from haunts of coot and hern,
  I make a sudden sally,
And sparkle out among the fern,
  To bicker down a valley.

By thirty hills I hurry down,
  Or slip between the ridges,
By twenty thorps, a little town,
  And half a hundred bridges.

Till last by Philip's farm I flow
  To join the brimming river,
For men may come and men may go,
  But I go on for ever.

I chatter over stony ways,
  In little sharps and trebles,
I bubble into eddying bays,
  I babble on the pebbles.

With many a curve my banks I fret
  By many a field and fallow,
And many a fairy foreland set
  With willow-weed and mallow.

I chatter, chatter, as I flow
  To join the brimming river,
For men may come and men may go,
  But I go on for ever.

I wind about, and in and out,
  With here a blossom sailing,
And here and there a lusty trout,
  And here and there a grayling.

And here and there a foamy flake
  Upon me, as I travel
With many a silvery water-break
  Above the golden gravel,

And draw them all along, and flow
  To join the brimming river,
For men may come and men may go,
  But I go on for ever.

I steal by lawns and grassy plots,
  I slide by hazel covers;
I move the sweet forget-me-nots
  That grow for happy lovers.

I slip, I slide, I gloom, I glance,
  Among my skimming swallows;
I make the netted sunbeam dance
  Against my sandy shallows.

I murmur under moon and stars
  In brambly wildernesses;
I linger by my shingly bars,
  I loiter round my cresses;

And out again I curve and flow
  To join the brimming river,
For men may come and men may go,
  But I go on for ever.

THE MILLER'S DAUGHTER

IT IS the miller's daughter,
  And she is grown so dear, so dear,
That I would be the jewel
  That trembles in her ear;
For hid in ringlets day and night,
I'd touch her neck so warm and white.

And I would be the girdle
  About her dainty dainty waist,
And her heart would beat against me,
  In sorrow and in rest;
And I should know if it beat right,
I'd clasp it round so close and tight.

And I would be the necklace,
  And all day long to fall and rise
Upon her balmy bosom,
  With her laughter or her sighs;
And I would lie so light, so light,
I scarce should be unclasp'd at night.

      Love that hath us in the net,
      Can he pass, and we forget?
      Many suns arise and set;
      Many a chance the years beget;
      Love the gift is Love the debt.
              Even so.

Love is hurt with jar and fret;
Love is made a vague regret;
Eyes with idle tears are wet;
Idle habit links us yet.
What is love? for we forget:
   Ah, no! no!

SEA DREAMS

WHAT does little birdie say
In her nest at peep of day?
Let me fly, says little birdie,
Mother, let me fly away.
Birdie, rest a little longer,
Till the little wings are stronger,
So she rests a little longer,
Then she flies away.

What does little baby say,
In her bed at peep of day?
Baby says, like little birdie,
Let me rise and fly away.
Baby, sleep a little longer,
Till the little limbs are stronger;
If she sleeps a little longer,
Baby too shall fly away.

ROMNEY'S REMORSE

'BEAT upon mine, little heart! beat, beat!
Beat upon mine! you are mine, my sweet!
All mine from your pretty blue eyes to your feet,
   My sweet.

'Sleep, little blossom, my honey, my bliss!
For I give you this, and I give you this!
And I blind your pretty blue eyes with a kiss!
          Sleep!

'Father and Mother will watch you grow,
And gather the roses whenever they blow,
And find the white heather wherever you go,
          My sweet.'

————

THE LOTOS-EATERS

THERE is sweet music here that softer falls
Than petals from blown roses on the grass,
Or night-dews on still waters between walls
Of shadowy granite, in a gleaming pass;
Music that gentlier on the spirit lies,
Than tired eyelids upon tired eyes;
Music that brings sweet sleep down from the blissful skies.
Here are cool mosses deep,
And thro' the moss the ivies creep,
And in the stream the long-leaved flowers weep,
And from the craggy ledge the poppy hangs in sleep.

Why are we weigh'd upon with heaviness,
And utterly consumed with sharp distress,
While all things else have rest from weariness?
All things have rest: why should we toil alone,
We only toil, who are the first of things,
And make perpetual moan,
Still from one sorrow to another thrown;
Nor ever fold our wings,

And cease from wanderings,
Nor steep our brows in slumber's holy balm;
Nor harken what the inner spirit sings,
'There is no joy but calm!'—
Why should we only toil, the roof and crown of things?

Lo! in the middle of the wood,
The folded leaf is woo'd from out the bud
With winds upon the branch, and there
Grows green and broad, and takes no care,
Sun-steep'd at noon, and in the moon
Nightly dew-fed; and turning yellow
Falls, and floats adown the air.
Lo! sweeten'd with the summer light,
The full-juiced apple, waxing over-mellow,
Drops in a silent autumn night.
All its allotted length of days
The flower ripens in its place,
Ripens and fades, and falls, and hath no toil,
Fast-rooted in the fruitful soil.

Hateful is the dark-blue sky,
Vaulted o'er the dark-blue sea.
Death is the end of life; ah, why
Should life all labor be?
Let us alone. Time driveth onward fast,
And in a little while our lips are dumb.
Let us alone. What is it that will last?
All things are taken from us, and become
Portions and parcels of the dreadful past.
Let us alone. What pleasure can we have
To war with evil? Is there any peace
In ever climbing up the climbing wave?
All things have rest, and ripen toward the grave

In silence—ripen, fall, and cease:
Give us long rest or death, dark death, or dreamful ease.

How sweet it were, hearing the downward stream,
With half-shut eyes ever to seem
Falling asleep in a half-dream!
To dream and dream, like yonder amber light,
Which will not leave the myrrh-bush on the height;
To hear each other's whisper'd speech;
Eating the Lotos day by day,
To watch the crisping ripples on the beach,
And tender curving lines of creamy spray;
To lend our hearts and spirits wholly
To the influence of mild-minded melancholy;
To muse and brood and live again in memory,
With those old faces of our infancy
Heap'd over with a mound of grass,
Two handfuls of white dust, shut in an urn of brass!

Dear is the memory of our wedded lives,
And dear the last embraces of our wives
And their warm tears; but all hath suffer'd change;
For surely now our household hearths are cold,
Our sons inherit us, our looks are strange,
And we should come like ghosts to trouble joy.
Or else the island princes over-bold
Have eat our substance, and the minstrel sings
Before them of the ten years' war in Troy,
And our great deeds, as half-forgotten things.
Is there confusion in the little isle?
Let what is broken so remain.
The Gods are hard to reconcile;
'T is hard to settle order once again.
There *is* confusion worse than death,

Trouble on trouble, pain on pain,
Long labor unto aged breath,
Sore task to hearts worn out by many wars
And eyes grown dim with gazing on the pilot-stars.

But, propt on beds of amaranth and moly,
How sweet—while warm airs lull us, blowing lowly—
With half-dropt eyelid still,
Beneath a heaven dark and holy,
To watch the long bright river drawing slowly
His waters from the purple hill—
To hear the dewy echoes calling
From cave to cave thro' the thick-twined vine—
To watch the emerald-color'd water falling
Thro' many a woven acanthus-wreath divine!
Only to hear and see the far-off sparkling brine,
Only to hear were sweet, stretch'd out beneath the pine.

The Lotos blooms below the barren peak,
The Lotos blows by every winding creek;
All day the wind breathes low with mellower tone;
Thro' every hollow cave and alley lone
Round and round the spicy downs the yellow Lotos-dust is
    blown.
We have had enough of action, and of motion we,
Roll'd to starboard, roll'd to larboard, when the surge was
    seething free,
Where the wallowing monster spouted his foam-fountains in
    the sea.
Let us swear an oath, and keep it with an equal mind,
In the hollow Lotos-land to live and lie reclined
On the hills like Gods together, careless of mankind.
For they lie beside their nectar, and the bolts are hurl'd

Far below them in the valleys, and the clouds are lightly
    curl'd
Round their golden houses, girdled with the gleaming world;
Where they smile in secret, looking over wasted lands,
Blight and famine, plague and earthquake, roaring deeps and
    fiery sands,
Clanging fights, and flaming towns, and sinking ships, and
    praying hands.
But they smile, they find a music centred in a doleful song
Steaming up, a lamentation and an ancient tale of wrong,
Like a tale of little meaning tho' the words are strong;
Chanted from an ill-used race of men that cleave the soil,
Sow the seed, and reap the harvest with enduring toil,
Storing yearly little dues of wheat, and wine and oil;
Till they perish and they suffer—some, 't is whisper'd—down
    in hell
Suffer endless anguish, others in Elysian valleys dwell,
Resting weary limbs at last on beds of asphodel.
Surely, surely, slumber is more sweet than toil, the shore
Than labor in the deep mid-ocean, wind and wave and oar;
O rest ye, brother mariners, we will not wander more.

ELEGIES

TO MY BROTHER CHARLES TENNYSON

MIDNIGHT, JUNE 30, 1879

MIDNIGHT—in no midsummer tune
The breakers lash the shores;
The cuckoo of a joyless June
Is calling out of doors.

And thou hast vanish'd from thine own
To that which looks like rest,
True brother, only to be known
By those who love thee best.

Midnight—and joyless June gone by,
And from the deluged park
The cuckoo of a worse July
Is calling thro' the dark;

But thou art silent underground,
And o'er thee streams the rain,
True poet, surely to be found
When Truth is found again.

And, now to these unsummer'd skies
The summer bird is still,
Far off a phantom cuckoo cries
From out a phantom hill;

And thro' this midnight breaks the sun
Of sixty years away,
The light of days when life begun,
The days that seem to-day,

When all my griefs were shared with thee,
As all my hopes were thine—
As all thou wert was one with me,
May all thou art be mine!

———————

IN MEMORIAM ARTHUR HENRY HALLAM

OBIT MDCCCXXXIII

STRONG Son of God, immortal Love,
    Whom we, that have not seen thy face,
    By faith, and faith alone, embrace,
Believing where we cannot prove;

Thine are these orbs of light and shade;
    Thou madest Life in man and brute;
    Thou madest Death; and lo, thy foot
Is on the skull which thou hast made.

Thou wilt not leave us in the dust:
    Thou madest man, he knows not why,
    He thinks he was not made to die;
And thou hast made him: thou art just

Thou seemest human and divine,
    The highest, holiest manhood, thou.
    Our wills are ours, we know not how;
Our wills are ours, to make them thine.

Our little systems have their day;
   They have their day and cease to be;
   They are but broken lights of thee,
And thou, O Lord, art more than they.

We have but faith: we cannot know,
   For knowledge is of things we see;
   And yet we trust it comes from thee,
A beam in darkness: let it grow.

Let knowledge grow from more to more,
   But more of reverence in us dwell;
   That mind and soul, according well,
May make one music as before,

But vaster. We are fools and slight;
   We mock thee when we do not fear:
   But help thy foolish ones to bear;
Help thy vain worlds to bear thy light.

Forgive what seem'd my sin in me,
   What seem'd my worth since I began;
   For merit lives from man to man,
And not from man, O Lord, to thee.

Forgive my grief for one removed,
   Thy creature, whom I found so fair.
   I trust he lives in thee, and there
I find him worthier to be loved.

Forgive these wild and wandering cries,
   Confusions of a wasted youth;
   Forgive them where they fail in truth,
And in thy wisdom make me wise.

   1849.

I

I held it truth, with him who sings
  To one clear harp in divers tones,
  That men may rise on stepping-stones
Of their dead selves to higher things.

But who shall so forecast the years
  And find in loss a gain to match?
  Or reach a hand thro' time to catch
The far-off interest of tears?

Let Love clasp Grief lest both be drown'd,
  Let darkness keep her raven gloss.
  Ah, sweeter to be drunk with loss,
To dance with Death, to beat the ground,

Than that the victor Hours should scorn
  The long result of love, and boast,
  'Behold the man that loved and lost
But all he was is overworn.'

II

Old yew, which graspest at the stones
  That name the underlying dead,
  Thy fibres net the dreamless head,
Thy roots are wrapt about the bones.

The seasons bring the flower again,
  And bring the firstling to the flock;
  And in the dusk of thee the clock
Beats out the little lives of men.

O, not for thee the glow, the bloom,
  Who changest not in any gale,
  Nor branding summer suns avail
To touch thy thousand years of gloom;

And gazing on thee, sullen tree,
  Sick for thy stubborn hardihood,
  I seem to fail from out my blood
And grow incorporate into thee.

III

O Sorrow, cruel fellowship,
  O Priestess in the vaults of Death,
  O sweet and bitter in a breath,
What whispers from thy lying lip?

'The stars,' she whispers, 'blindly run;
  A web is woven across the sky;
  From out waste places comes a cry,
And murmurs from the dying sun;

'And all the phantom, Nature, stands—
  With all the music in her tone,
  A hollow echo of my own,—
A hollow form with empty hands.'

And shall I take a thing so blind,
  Embrace her as my natural good;
  Or crush her, like a vice of blood,
Upon the threshold of the mind?

IV

To Sleep I give my powers away;
  My will is bondsman to the dark;
  I sit within a helmless bark,
And with my heart I muse and say:

O heart, how fares it with thee now,
  That thou shouldst fail from thy desire,
  Who scarcely darest to inquire,
'What is it makes me beat so low?'

Something it is which thou hast lost,
  Some pleasure from thine early years.
  Break, thou deep vase of chilling tears,
That grief hath shaken into frost!

Such clouds of nameless trouble cross
  All night below the darken'd eyes;
  With morning wakes the will, and cries,
'Thou shalt not be the fool of loss.'

V

I sometimes hold it half a sin
  To put in words the grief I feel;
  For words, like Nature, half reveal
And half conceal the Soul within.

But, for the unquiet heart and brain,
  A use in measured language lies;
  The sad mechanic exercise,
Like dull narcotics, numbing pain.

In words, like weeds, I'll wrap me o'er,
  Like coarsest clothes against the cold;
  But that large grief which these enfold
Is given in outline and no more.

VI

One writes, that 'other friends remain,'
  That 'loss is common to the race'—
  And common is the commonplace,
And vacant chaff well meant for grain.

That loss is common would not make
  My own less bitter, rather more.
  Too common! Never morning wore
To evening, but some heart did break.

O father, wheresoe'er thou be,
  Who pledgest now thy gallant son,
  A shot, ere half thy draught be done,
Hath still'd the life that beat from thee.

O mother, praying God will save
  Thy sailor,—while thy head is bow'd,
  His heavy-shotted hammock-shroud
Drops in his vast and wandering grave.

Ye know no more than I who wrought
  At that last hour to please him well;
  Who mused on all I had to tell,
And something written, something thought;

Expecting still his advent home;
　And ever met him on his way
　With wishes, thinking, 'here to-day,'
Or 'here to-morrow will he come.'

O, somewhere, meek, unconscious dove,
　That sittest ranging golden hair;
　And glad to find thyself so fair,
Poor child, that waitest for thy love!

For now her father's chimney glows
　In expectation of a guest;
　And thinking 'this will please him best,'
She takes a riband or a rose;

For he will see them on to-night;
　And with the thought her color burns;
　And, having left the glass, she turns
Once more to set a ringlet right;

And, even when she turn'd, the curse
　Had fallen, and her future lord
　Was drown'd in passing thro' the ford,
Or kill'd in falling from his horse.

O, what to her shall be the end?
　And what to me remains of good?
　To her perpetual maidenhood,
And unto me no second friend.

VII

Dark house, by which once more I stand
　Here in the long unlovely street,
　Doors, where my heart was used to beat
So quickly, waiting for a hand,

A hand that can be clasp'd no more—
  Behold me, for I cannot sleep,
  And like a guilty thing I creep
At earliest morning to the door.

He is not here; but far away
  The noise of life begins again,
  And ghastly thro' the drizzling rain
On the bald street breaks the blank day.

VIII

A happy lover who has come
  To look on her that loves him well,
  Who 'lights and rings the gateway bell,
And learns her gone and far from home;

He saddens, all the magic light
  Dies off at once from bower and hall,
  And all the place is dark, and all
The chambers emptied of delight:

So find I every pleasant spot
  In which we two were wont to meet,
  The field, the chamber, and the street,
For all is dark where thou art not.

Yet as that other, wandering there
  In those deserted walks, may find
  A flower beat with rain and wind,
Which once she foster'd up with care;

So seems it in my deep regret,
  O my forsaken heart, with thee
  And this poor flower of poesy
Which, little cared for, fades not yet.

But since it pleased a vanish'd eye,
 I go to plant it on his tomb,
 That if it can it there may bloom,
Or, dying, there at least may die.

IX

Fair ship, that from the Italian shore
 Sailest the placid ocean-plains
 With my lost Arthur's loved remains,
Spread thy full wings, and waft him o'er.

So draw him home to those that mourn
 In vain; a favorable speed
 Ruffle thy mirror'd mast, and lead
Thro' prosperous floods his holy urn.

All night no ruder air perplex
 Thy sliding keel, till Phosphor, bright
 As our pure love, thro' early light
Shall glimmer on the dewy decks.

Sphere all your lights around, above;
 Sleep, gentle heavens, before the prow;
 Sleep, gentle winds, as he sleeps now,
My friend, the brother of my love;

My Arthur, whom I shall not see
 Till all my widow'd race be run;
 Dear as the mother to the son,
More than my brothers are to me.

X

I hear the noise about thy keel;
  I hear the bell struck in the night;
  I see the cabin-window bright;
I see the sailor at the wheel.

Thou bring'st the sailor to his wife,
  And travell'd men from foreign lands;
  And letters unto trembling hands;
And, thy dark freight, a vanish'd life.

So bring him; we have idle dreams;
  This look of quiet flatters thus
  Our home-bred fancies. O, to us,
The fools of habit, sweeter seems

To rest beneath the clover sod,
  That takes the sunshine and the rains,
  Or where the kneeling hamlet drains
The chalice of the grapes of God;

Than if with thee the roaring wells
  Should gulf him fathom-deep in brine,
  And hands so often clasp'd in mine,
Should toss with tangle and with shells.

XI

Calm is the morn without a sound,
  Calm as to suit a calmer grief,
  And only thro' the faded leaf
The chestnut pattering to the ground;

Calm and deep peace on this high wold,
  And on these dews that drench the furze,
  And all the silvery gossamers
That twinkle into green and gold;

Calm and still light on yon great plain
  That sweeps with all its autumn bowers,
  And crowded farms and lessening towers,
To mingle with the bounding main;

Calm and deep peace in this wide air,
  These leaves that redden to the fall,
  And in my heart, if calm at all,
If any calm, a calm despair;

Calm on the seas, and silver sleep,
  And waves that sway themselves in rest,
  And dead calm in that noble breast
Which heaves but with the heaving deep.

XII

Lo, as a dove when up she springs
  To bear thro' heaven a tale of woe,
  Some dolorous message knit below
The wild pulsation of her wings;

Like her I go, I cannot stay;
  I leave this mortal ark behind,
  A weight of nerves without a mind,
And leave the cliffs, and haste away

O'er ocean-mirrors rounded large,
  And reach the glow of southern skies,
  And see the sails at distance rise,
And linger weeping on the marge,

And saying, 'Comes he thus, my friend?
  Is this the end of all my care?
  And circle moaning in the air,
Is this the end? Is this the end?'

And forward dart again, and play
  About the prow, and back return
  To where the body sits, and learn
That I have been an hour away.

XIII

Tears of the widower, when he sees
  A late-lost form that sleep reveals,
  And moves his doubtful arms, and feels
Her place is empty, fall like these;

Which weep a loss for ever new,
  A void where heart on heart reposed;
  And, where warm hands have prest and closed,
Silence, till I be silent too;

Which weep the comrade of my choice,
  An awful thought, a life removed,
  The human-hearted man I loved,
A Spirit, not a breathing voice.

Come, Time, and teach me, many years,
    I do not suffer in a dream;
    For now so strange do these things seem,
Mine eyes have leisure for their tears,

My fancies time to rise on wing,
    And glance about the approaching sails,
    As tho' they brought but merchants' bales,
And not the burthen that they bring.

XIV

If one should bring me this report,
    That thou hadst touch'd the land to-day,
    And I went down unto the quay,
And found thee lying in the port;

And standing, muffled round with woe,
    Should see thy passengers in rank
    Come stepping lightly down the plank,
And beckoning unto those they know;

And if along with these should come
    The man I held as half-divine,
    Should strike a sudden hand in mine,
And ask a thousand things of home;

And I should tell him all my pain,
    And how my life had droop'd of late,
    And he should sorrow o'er my state
And marvel what possess'd my brain;

And I perceived no touch of change,
  No hint of death in all his frame,
  But found him all in all the same,
I should not feel it to be strange.

XV

To-night the winds begin to rise
  And roar from yonder dropping day;
  The last red leaf is whirl'd away,
The rooks are blown about the skies;

The forest crack'd, the waters curl'd,
  The cattle huddled on the lea;
  And wildly dash'd on tower and tree
The sunbeam strikes along the world:

And but for fancies, which aver
  That all thy motions gently pass
  Athwart a plane of molten glass,
I scarce could brook the strain and stir

That makes the barren branches loud;
  And but for fear it is not so,
  The wild unrest that lives in woe
Would dote and pore on yonder cloud

That rises upward always higher,
  And onward drags a laboring breast,
  And topples round the dreary west,
A looming bastion fringed with fire.

XVI

What words are these have fallen from me?
    Can calm despair and wild unrest
    Be tenants of a single breast,
Or Sorrow such a changeling be?

Or doth she only seem to take
    The touch of change in calm or storm,
    But knows no more of transient form
In her deep self, than some dead lake

That holds the shadow of a lark
    Hung in the shadow of a heaven?
    Or has the shock, so harshly given,
Confused me like the unhappy bark

That strikes by night a craggy shelf,
    And staggers blindly ere she sink?
    And stunn'd me from my power to think
And all my knowledge of myself;

And made me that delirious man
    Whose fancy fuses old and new,
    And flashes into false and true,
And mingles all without a plan?

XVII

Thou comest, much wept for; such a breeze
    Compell'd thy canvas, and my prayer
    Was as the whisper of an air
To breathe thee over lonely seas.

For I in spirit saw thee move
  Thro' circles of the bounding sky,
  Week after week; the days go by;
Come quick, thou bringest all I love.

Henceforth, wherever thou mayst roam,
  My blessing, like a line of light,
  Is on the waters day and night,
And like a beacon guards thee home.

So may whatever tempest mars
  Mid-ocean spare thee, sacred bark,
  And balmy drops in summer dark
Slide from the bosom of the stars;

So kind an office hath been done,
  Such precious relics brought by thee,
  The dust of him I shall not see
Till all my widow'd race be run.

XVIII

'T is well; 't is something; we may stand
  Where he in English earth is laid,
  And from his ashes may be made
The violet of his native land.

'T is little; but it looks in truth
  As if the quiet bones were blest
  Among familiar names to rest
And in the places of his youth.

Come then, pure hands, and bear the head
  That sleeps or wears the mask of sleep,
  And come, whatever loves to weep,
And hear the ritual of the dead.

Ah yet, even yet, if this might be,
  I, falling on his faithful heart,
  Would breathing thro' his lips impart
The life that almost dies in me;

That dies not, but endures with pain,
  And slowly forms the firmer mind,
  Treasuring the look it cannot find,
The words that are not heard again.

XIX

The Danube to the Severn gave
  The darken'd heart that beat no more;
  They laid him by the pleasant shore,
And in the hearing of the wave.

There twice a day the Severn fills;
  The salt sea-water passes by,
  And hushes half the babbling Wye,
And makes a silence in the hills.

The Wye is hush'd nor moved along,
  And hush'd my deepest grief of all,
  When fill'd with tears that cannot fall,
I brim with sorrow drowning song.

The tide flows down, the wave again
  Is vocal in its wooded walls;
  My deeper anguish also falls,
And I can speak a little then.

XX

The lesser griefs that may be said,
  That breathe a thousand tender vows,
  Are but as servants in a house
Where lies the master newly dead;

Who speak their feeling as it is,
  And weep the fulness from the mind.
  'It will be hard,' they say, 'to find
Another service such as this.'

My lighter moods are like to these,
  That out of words a comfort win;
  But there are other griefs within,
And tears that at their fountain freeze;

For by the hearth the children sit
  Cold in that atmosphere of death,
  And scarce endure to draw the breath,
Or like to noiseless phantoms flit;

But open converse is there none,
  So much the vital spirits sink
  To see the vacant chair, and think,
'How good! how kind! and he is gone.'

XXI

I sing to him that rests below,
  And, since the grasses round me wave,
  I take the grasses of the grave,
And make them pipes whereon to blow.

The traveller hears me now and then,
  And sometimes harshly will he speak:
  'This fellow would make weakness weak,
And melt the waxen hearts of men.'

Another answers: 'Let him be,
  He loves to make parade of pain,
  That with his piping he may gain
The praise that comes to constancy.'

A third is wroth: 'Is this an hour
  For private sorrow's barren song,
  When more and more the people throng
The chairs and thrones of civil power?

'A time to sicken and to swoon,
  When Science reaches forth her arms
  To feel from world to world, and charms
Her secret from the latest moon?

Behold, ye speak an idle thing;
  Ye never knew the sacred dust.
  I do but sing because I must,
And pipe but as the linnets sing;

And one is glad; her note is gay,
 For now her little ones have ranged;
 And one is sad; her note is changed,
Because her brood is stolen away.

XXII

The path by which we twain did go,
 Which led by tracts that pleased us well,
 Thro' four sweet years arose and fell,
From flower to flower, from snow to snow;

And we with singing cheer'd the way,
 And, crown'd with all the season lent,
 From April on to April went,
And glad at heart from May to May.

But where the path we walk'd began
 To slant the fifth autumnal slope,
 As we descended following Hope,
There sat the Shadow fear'd of man;

Who broke our fair companionship,
 And spread his mantle dark and cold,
 And wrapt thee formless in the fold,
And dull'd the murmur on thy lip,

And bore thee where I could not see
 Nor follow, tho' I walk in haste,
 And think that somewhere in the waste
The Shadow sits and waits for me.

XXIII

Now, sometimes in my sorrow shut,
  Or breaking into song by fits,
  Alone, alone, to where he sits,
The Shadow cloak'd from head to foot,

Who keeps the keys of all the creeds,
  I wander, often falling lame,
  And looking back to whence I came,
Or on to where the pathway leads;

And crying, How changed from where it ran
  Thro' lands where not a leaf was dumb,
  But all the lavish hills would hum
The murmur of a happy Pan;

When each by turns was guide to each,
  And Fancy light from Fancy caught,
  And Thought leapt out to wed with Thought
Ere Thought could wed itself with Speech;

And all we met was fair and good,
  And all was good that Time could bring,
  And all the secret of the Spring
Moved in the chambers of the blood;

And many an old philosophy
  On Argive heights divinely sang,
  And round us all the thicket rang
To many a flute of Arcady.

XXIV

And was the day of my delight
　　As pure and perfect as I say?
　　The very source and fount of day
Is dash'd with wandering isles of night.

If all was good and fair we met,
　　This earth had been the Paradise
　　It never look'd to human eyes
Since our first sun arose and set.

And is it that the haze of grief
　　Makes former gladness loom so great?
　　The lowness of the present state,
That sets the past in this relief?

Or that the past will always win
　　A glory from its being far,
　　And orb into the perfect star
We saw not when we moved therein?

XXV

I know that this was Life,—the track
　　Whereon with equal feet we fared;
　　And then, as now, the day prepared
The daily burden for the back.

But this it was that made me move
　　As light as carrier-birds in air;
　　I loved the weight I had to bear,
Because it needed help of Love;

Nor could I weary, heart or limb,
  When mighty Love would cleave in twain
  The lading of a single pain,
And part it, giving half to him.

XXVI

Still onward winds the dreary way;
  I with it, for I long to prove
  No lapse of moons can canker Love,
Whatever fickle tongues may say.

And if that eye which watches guilt
  And goodness, and hath power to see
  Within the green the moulder'd tree,
And towers fallen as soon as built—

O, if indeed that eye foresee
  Or see—in Him is no before—
  In more of life true life no more
And Love the indifference to be,

Then might I find, ere yet the morn
  Breaks hither over Indian seas,
  That Shadow waiting with the keys,
To shroud me from my proper scorn.

XXVII

I envy not in any moods
  The captive void of noble rage,
  The linnet born within the cage,
That never knew the summer woods;

I envy not the beast that takes
  His license in the field of time,
  Unfetter'd by the sense of crime,
To whom a conscience never wakes;

Nor, what may count itself as blest,
  The heart that never plighted troth
  But stagnates in the weeds of sloth;
Nor any want-begotten rest.

I hold it true, whate'er befall;
  I feel it, when I sorrow most;
  'T is better to have loved and lost
Than never to have loved at all.

XXVIII

The time draws near the birth of Christ.
  The moon is hid, the night is still;
  The Christmas bells from hill to hill
Answer each other in the mist.

Four voices of four hamlets round,
  From far and near, on mead and moor,
  Swell out and fail, as if a door
Were shut between me and the sound;

Each voice four changes on the wind,
  That now dilate, and now decrease,
  Peace and goodwill, goodwill and peace,
Peace and goodwill, to all mankind.

This year I slept and woke with pain,
    I almost wish'd no more to wake,
    And that my hold on life would break
Before I heard those bells again;

But they my troubled spirit rule,
    For they controll'd me when a boy;
    They bring me sorrow touch'd with joy,
The merry, merry bells of Yule.

XXIX

With such compelling cause to grieve
    As daily vexes household peace,
    And chains regret to his decease,
How dare we keep our Christmas-eve,

Which brings no more a welcome guest
    To enrich the threshold of the night
    With shower'd largess of delight
In dance and song and game and jest?

Yet go, and while the holly boughs
    Entwine the cold baptismal font,
    Make one wreath more for Use and Wont,
That guard the portals of the house;

Old sisters of a day gone by,
    Gray nurses, loving nothing new—
    Why should they miss their yearly due
Before their time? They too will die.

XXX

With trembling fingers did we weave
 The holly round the Christmas hearth;
 A rainy cloud possess'd the earth,
And sadly fell our Christmas-eve.

At our old pastimes in the hall
 We gamboll'd, making vain pretence
 Of gladness, with an awful sense
Of one mute Shadow watching all.

We paused: the winds were in the beech:
 We heard them sweep the winter land;
 And in a circle hand-in-hand
Sat silent, looking each at each.

Then echo-like our voices rang;
 We sung, tho' every eye was dim,
 A merry song we sang with him
Last year; impetuously we sang.

We ceased; a gentler feeling crept
 Upon us: surely rest is meet.
 'They rest,' we said, 'their sleep is sweet,'
And silence follow'd, and we wept.

Our voices took a higher range;
 Once more we sang: 'They do not die
 Nor lose their mortal sympathy,
Nor change to us, although they change;

'Rapt from the fickle and the frail
  With gather'd power, yet the same,
  Pierces the keen seraphic flame
From orb to orb, from veil to veil.'

Rise, happy morn, rise, holy morn,
  Draw forth the cheerful day from night:
  O Father, touch the east, and light
The light that shone when Hope was born.

XXXI

When Lazarus left his charnel-cave,
  And home to Mary's house return'd,
  Was this demanded—if he yearn'd
To hear her weeping by his grave?

'Where wert thou, brother, those four days?'
  There lives no record of reply,
  Which telling what it is to die
Had surely added praise to praise.

From every house the neighbors met,
  The streets were fill'd with joyful sound,
  A solemn gladness even crown'd
The purple brows of Olivet.

Behold a man raised up by Christ!
  The rest remaineth unreveal'd;
  He told it not, or something seal'd
The lips of that Evangelist.

XXXII

Her eyes are homes of silent prayer,
  Nor other thought her mind admits
  But, he was dead, and there he sits,
And he that brought him back is there.

Then one deep love doth supersede
  All other, when her ardent gaze
  Roves from the living brother's face,
And rests upon the Life indeed.

All subtle thought, all curious fears,
  Borne down by gladness so complete,
  She bows, she bathes the Saviour's feet
With costly spikenard and with tears.

Thrice blest whose lives are faithful prayers,
  Whose loves in higher love endure;
  What souls possess themselves so pure,
Or is there blessedness like theirs?

XXXIII

O thou that after toil and storm
  Mayst seem to have reach'd a purer air,
  Whose faith has centre everywhere,
Nor cares to fix itself to form,

Leave thou thy sister when she prays
  Her early heaven, her happy views;
  Nor thou with shadow'd hint confuse
A life that leads melodious days.

Her faith thro' form is pure as thine,
  Her hands are quicker unto good.
  O, sacred be the flesh and blood
To which she links a truth divine!

See thou, that countest reason ripe
  In holding by the law within,
  Thou fail not in a world of sin,
And even for want of such a type.

XXXIV

My own dim life should teach me this,
  That life shall live for evermore,
  Else earth is darkness at the core,
And dust and ashes all that is;

This round of green, this orb of flame,
  Fantastic beauty; such as lurks
  In some wild poet, when he works
Without a conscience or an aim.

What then were God to such as I?
  'T were hardly worth my while to choose
  Of things all mortal, or to use
A little patience ere I die;

'T were best at once to sink to peace,
  Like birds the charming serpent draws,
  To drop head-foremost in the jaws
Of vacant darkness and to cease.

XXXV

Yet if some voice that man could trust
  Should murmur from the narrow house,
  'The cheeks drop in, the body bows;
Man dies, nor is there hope in dust;'

Might I not say? 'Yet even here,
  But for one hour, O Love, I strive
  To keep so sweet a thing alive.'
But I should turn mine ears and hear

The moanings of the homeless sea,
  The sound of streams that swift or slow
  Draw down Æonian hills, and sow
The dust of continents to be;

And Love would answer with a sigh,
  'The sound of that forgetful shore
  Will change my sweetness more and more,
Half-dead to know that I shall die.'

O me, what profits it to put
  An idle case? If Death were seen
  At first as Death, Love had not been,
Or been in narrowest working shut,

Mere fellowship of sluggish moods,
  Or in his coarsest Satyr-shape
  Had bruised the herb and crush'd the grape,
And bask'd and batten'd in the woods.

XXXVI

Tho' truths in manhood darkly join,
  Deep-seated in our mystic frame,
  We yield all blessing to the name
Of Him that made them current coin;

For Wisdom dealt with mortal powers,
  Where truth in closest words shall fail,
  When truth embodied in a tale
Shall enter in at lowly doors.

And so the Word had breath, and wrought
  With human hands the creed of creeds
  In loveliness of perfect deeds,
More strong than all poetic thought;

Which he may read that binds the sheaf,
  Or builds the house, or digs the grave,
  And those wild eyes that watch the wave
In roarings round the coral reef.

XXXVII

Urania speaks with darken'd brow:
  'Thou pratest here where thou art least;
  This faith has many a purer priest,
And many an abler voice than thou.

'Go down beside thy native rill,
  On thy Parnassus set thy feet,
  And hear thy laurel whisper sweet
About the ledges of the hill.'

And my Melpomene replies,
  A touch of shame upon her cheek:
  'I am not worthy even to speak
Of thy prevailing mysteries;

'For I am but an earthly Muse,
  And owning but a little art
  To lull with song an aching heart,
And render human love his dues;

'But brooding on the dear one dead,
  And all he said of things divine,—
  And dear to me as sacred wine
To dying lips is all he said,—

'I murmur'd, as I came along,
  Of comfort clasp'd in truth reveal'd,
  And loiter'd in the master's field,
And darken'd sanctities with song.'

XXXVIII

With weary steps I loiter on,
  Tho' always under alter'd skies
  The purple from the distance dies,
My prospect and horizon gone.

No joy the blowing season gives,
  The herald melodies of spring,
  But in the songs I love to sing
A doubtful gleam of solace lives.

If any care for what is here
　　Survive in spirits render'd free,
　　Then are these songs I sing of thee
Not all ungrateful to thine ear.

XXXIX

Old warder of these buried bones,
　　And answering now my random stroke
　　With fruitful cloud and living smoke,
Dark yew, that graspest at the stones

And dippest toward the dreamless head,
　　To thee too comes the golden hour
　　When flower is feeling after flower;
But Sorrow,—fixt upon the dead,

And darkening the dark graves of men,—
　　What whisper'd from her lying lips?
　　Thy gloom is kindled at the tips,
And passes into gloom again.

XL

Could we forget the widow'd hour
　　And look on Spirits breathed away,
　　As on a maiden in the day
When first she wears her orange-flower!

When crown'd with blessing she doth rise
　　To take her latest leave of home,
　　And hopes and light regrets that come
Make April of her tender eyes;

And doubtful joys the father move,
  And tears are on the mother's face,
  As parting with a long embrace
She enters other realms of love;

Her office there to rear, to teach,
  Becoming as is meet and fit
  A link among the days, to knit
The generations each with each;

And, doubtless, unto thee is given
  A life that bears immortal fruit
  In those great offices that suit
The full-grown energies of heaven.

Ay me, the difference I discern!
  How often shall her old fireside
  Be cheer'd with tidings of the bride,
How often she herself return,

And tell them all they would have told,
  And bring her babe, and make her boast,
  Till even those that miss'd her most
Shall count new things as dear as old;

But thou and I have shaken hands,
  Till growing winters lay me low;
  My paths are in the fields I know,
And thine in undiscover'd lands.

XLI

Thy spirit ere our fatal loss
  Did ever rise from high to higher,
  As mounts the heavenward altar-fire,
As flies the lighter thro' the gross.

But thou art turn'd to something strange,
　And I have lost the links that bound
　Thy changes; here upon the ground,
No more partaker of thy change.

Deep folly! yet that this could be—
　That I could wing my will with might
　To leap the grades of life and light,
And flash at once, my friend, to thee!

For tho' my nature rarely yields
　To that vague fear implied in death,
　Nor shudders at the gulfs beneath,
The howlings from forgotten fields;

Yet oft when sundown skirts the moor
　An inner trouble I behold,
　A spectral doubt which makes me cold,
That I shall be thy mate no more,

Tho' following with an upward mind
　The wonders that have come to thee,
　Thro' all the secular to-be,
But evermore a life behind.

XLII

I vex my heart with fancies dim.
　He still outstript me in the race;
　It was but unity of place
That made me dream I rank'd with him.

And so may Place retain us still,
   And he the much-beloved again,
   A lord of large experience, train
To riper growth the mind and will;

And what delights can equal those
   That stir the spirit's inner deeps,
   When one that loves, but knows not, reaps
A truth from one that loves and knows?

XLIII

If Sleep and Death be truly one,
   And every spirit's folded bloom
   Thro' all its intervital gloom
In some long trance should slumber on;

Unconscious of the sliding hour,
   Bare of the body, might it last,
   And silent traces of the past
Be all the color of the flower:

So then were nothing lost to man;
   So that still garden of the souls
   In many a figured leaf enrolls
The total world since life began;

And love will last as pure and whole
   As when he loved me here in Time
   And at the spiritual prime
Rewaken with the dawning soul.

XLIV

How fares it with the happy dead?
  For here the man is more and more:
  But he forgets the days before
God shut the doorways of his head.

The days have vanish'd, tone and tint,
  And yet perhaps the hoarding sense
  Gives out at times—he knows not whence—
A little flash, a mystic hint;

And in the long harmonious years—
  If Death so taste Lethean springs—
  May some dim touch of earthly things
Surprise thee ranging with thy peers.

If such a dreamy touch should fall,
  O, turn thee round, resolve the doubt;
  My guardian angel will speak out
In that high place, and tell thee all.

XLV

The baby new to earth and sky,
  What time his tender palm is prest
  Against the circle of the breast,
Has never thought that 'this is I;'

But as he grows he gathers much,
  And learns the use of 'I' and 'me,'
  And finds 'I am not what I see,
And other than the things I touch.'

So rounds he to a separate mind
From whence clear memory may begin,
As thro' the frame that binds him in
His isolation grows defined.

This use may lie in blood and breath,
Which else were fruitless of their due,
Had man to learn himself anew
Beyond the second birth of death.

XLVI

We ranging down this lower track,
The path we came by, thorn and flower,
Is shadow'd by the growing hour,
Lest life should fail in looking back.

So be it: there no shade can last
In that deep dawn behind the tomb,
But clear from marge to marge shall bloom
The eternal landscape of the past;

A lifelong tract of time reveal'd,
The fruitful hours of still increase;
Days order'd in a wealthy peace,
And those five years its richest field.

O love, thy province were not large,
A bounded field, nor stretching far;
Look also, Love, a brooding star,
A rosy warmth from marge to marge.

XLVII

That each, who seems a separate whole,
    Should move his rounds, and fusing all
    The skirts of self again, should fall
Remerging in the general Soul,

Is faith as vague as all unsweet.
    Eternal form shall still divide
    The eternal soul from all beside;
And I shall know him when we meet;

And we shall sit at endless feast,
    Enjoying each the other's good.
    What vaster dream can hit the mood
Of Love on earth? He seeks at least

Upon the last and sharpest height,
    Before the spirits fade away,
    Some landing-place, to clasp and say,
'Farewell! We lose ourselves in light.'

XLVIII

If these brief lays, of Sorrow born,
    Were taken to be such as closed
    Grave doubts and answers here proposed,
Then these were such as men might scorn.

Her care is not to part and prove;
    She takes, when harsher moods remit.
    What slender shade of doubt may flit,
And makes it vassal unto love;

And hence, indeed, she sports with words,
  But better serves a wholesome law,
  And holds it sin and shame to draw
The deepest measure from the chords;

Nor dare she trust a larger lay,
  But rather loosens from the lip
  Short swallow-flights of song, that dip
Their wings in tears, and skim away.

XLIX

From art, from nature, from the schools,
  Let random influences glance,
  Like light in many a shiver'd lance
That breaks about the dappled pools.

The lightest wave of thought shall lisp,
  The fancy's tenderest eddy wreathe,
  The slightest air of song shall breathe
To make the sullen surface crisp.

And look thy look, and go thy way,
  But blame not thou the winds that make
  The seeming-wanton ripple break,
The tender-pencill'd shadow play.

Beneath all fancied hopes and fears
  Ay me, the sorrow deepens down,
  Whose muffled motions blindly drown
The bases of my life in tears.

L

Be near me when my light is low,
  When the blood creeps, and the nerves prick
  And tingle; and the heart is sick,
And all the wheels of being slow.

Be near me when the sensuous frame
  Is rack'd with pangs that conquer trust;
  And Time, a maniac scattering dust,
And Life, a Fury slinging flame.

Be near me when my faith is dry,
  And men the flies of latter spring,
  That lay their eggs, and sting and sing
And weave their petty cells and die.

Be near me when I fade away,
  To point the term of human strife,
  And on the low dark verge of life
The twilight of eternal day.

LI

Do we indeed desire the dead
  Should still be near us at our side?
  Is there no baseness we would hide?
No inner vileness that we dread?

Shall he for whose applause I strove,
  I had such reverence for his blame,
  See with clear eye some hidden shame
And I be lessen'd in his love?

I wrong the grave with fears untrue.
   Shall love be blamed for want of faith?
   There must be wisdom with great Death;
The dead shall look me thro' and thro'.

Be near us when we climb or fall;
   Ye watch, like God, the rolling hours
   With larger other eyes than ours,
To make allowance for us all.

LII

I cannot love thee as I ought,
   For love reflects the thing beloved;
   My words are only words, and moved
Upon the topmost froth of thought.

'Yet blame not thou thy plaintive song,'
   The Spirit of true love replied;
   'Thou canst not move me from thy side,
Nor human frailty do me wrong.

'What keeps a spirit wholly true
   To that ideal which he bears?
   What record? not the sinless years
That breathed beneath the Syrian blue;

'So fret not, like an idle girl,
   That life is dash'd with flecks of sin.
   Abide; thy wealth is gather'd in,
When Time hath sunder'd shell from pearl.'

How many a father have I seen,
  A sober man, among his boys,
  Whose youth was full of foolish noise,
Who wears his manhood hale and green;

And dare we to this fancy give,
  That had the wild oat not been sown,
  The soil, left barren, scarce had grown
The grain by which a man may live?

Or, if we held the doctrine sound
  For life outliving heats of youth,
  Yet who would preach it as a truth
To those that eddy round and round?

Hold thou the good, define it well;
  For fear divine Philosophy
  Should push beyond her mark, and be
Procuress to the Lords of Hell.

O, yet we trust that somehow good
  Will be the final goal of ill,
  To pangs of nature, sins of will,
Defects of doubt, and taints of blood;

That nothing walks with aimless feet;
  That not one life shall be destroy'd,
  Or cast as rubbish to the void,
When God hath made the pile complete;

That not a worm is cloven in vain;
  That not a moth with vain desire
  Is shrivell'd in a fruitless fire,
Or but subserves another's gain.

Behold, we know not anything;
  I can but trust that good shall fall
  At last—far off—at last, to all,
And every winter change to spring.

So runs my dream; but what am I?
  An infant crying in the night;
  An infant crying for the light,
And with no language but a cry.

LV

The wish, that of the living whole
  No life may fail beyond the grave,
  Derives it not from what we have
The likest God within the soul?

Are God and Nature then at strife,
  That Nature lends such evil dreams?
  So careful of the type she seems,
So careless of the single life,

That I, considering everywhere
  Her secret meaning in her deeds,
  And finding that of fifty seeds
She often brings but one to bear,

I falter where I firmly trod,
  And falling with my weight of cares
  Upon the great world's altar-stairs
That slope thro' darkness up to God,

I stretch lame hands of faith, and grope,
  And gather dust and chaff, and call
  To what I feel is Lord of all,
And faintly trust the larger hope.

LVI

'So careful of the type?' but no.
  From scarped cliff and quarried stone
  She cries, 'A thousand types are gone;
I care for nothing, all shall go.

'Thou makest thine appeal to me:
  I bring to life, I bring to death;
  The spirit does but mean the breath:
I know no more.' And he, shall he,

Man, her last work, who seem'd so fair,
  Such splendid purpose in his eyes,
  Who roll'd the psalm to wintry skies,
Who built him fanes of fruitless prayer,

Who trusted God was love indeed
  And love Creation's final law—
  Tho' Nature, red in tooth and claw
With ravine, shriek'd against his creed—

Who loved, who suffer'd countless ills,
　Who battled for the True, the Just,
　Be blown about the desert dust,
Or seal'd within the iron hills?

No more? A monster then, a dream,
　A discord. Dragons of the prime,
　That tare each other in their slime,
Were mellow music match'd with him.

O life as futile, then, as frail!
　O for thy voice to soothe and bless
　What hope of answer, or redress?
Behind the veil, behind the veil.

LVII

Peace; come away: the song of woe
　Is after all an earthly song.
　Peace; come away: we do him wrong
To sing so wildly: let us go.

Come; let us go: your cheeks are pale;
　But half my life I leave behind.
　Methinks my friend is richly shrined;
But I shall pass, my work will fail.

Yet in these ears, till hearing dies,
　One set slow bell will seem to toll
　The passing of the sweetest soul
That ever look'd with human eyes.

I hear it now, and o'er and o'er,
　Eternal greetings to the dead;
　And 'Ave, Ave, Ave,' said,
'Adieu, adieu,' for evermore.

LVIII

In those sad words I took farewell.
　Like echoes in sepulchral halls,
　As drop by drop the water falls
In vaults and catacombs, they fell;

And, falling, idly broke the peace
　Of hearts that beat from day to day,
　Half-conscious of their dying clay,
And those cold crypts where they shall cease.

The high Muse answer'd: 'Wherefore grieve
　Thy brethren with a fruitless tear?
　Abide a little longer here,
And thou shalt take a nobler leave.'

LIX

O Sorrow, wilt thou live with me
　No casual mistress, but a wife,
　My bosom-friend and half of life;
As I confess it needs must be?

O Sorrow, wilt thou rule my blood,
　Be sometimes lovely like a bride,
　And put thy harsher moods aside,
If thou wilt have me wise and good?

My centred passion cannot move,
  Nor will it lessen from to-day;
  But I 'll have leave at times to play
As with the creature of my love;

And set thee forth, for thou art mine,
  With so much hope for years to come,
  That, howsoe'er I know thee, some
Could hardly tell what name were thine.

LX

He past, a soul of nobler tone;
  My spirit loved and loves him yet,
  Like some poor girl whose heart is set
On one whose rank exceeds her own.

He mixing with his proper sphere,
  She finds the baseness of her lot,
  Half jealous of she knows not what,
And envying all that meet him there.

The little village looks forlorn;
  She sighs amid her narrow days,
  Moving about the household ways,
In that dark house where she was born.

The foolish neighbors come and go,
  And tease her till the day draws by;
  At night she weeps, 'How vain am I!
How should he love a thing so low?'

LXI

If, in thy second state sublime,
  Thy ransom'd reason change replies
  With all the circle of the wise,
The perfect flower of human time;

And if thou cast thine eyes below,
  How dimly character'd and slight,
  How dwarf'd a growth of cold and night,
How blanch'd with darkness must I grow!

Yet turn thee to the doubtful shore,
  Where thy first form was made a man;
  I loved thee, Spirit, and love, nor can
The soul of Shakespeare love thee more.

LXII

Tho' if an eye that 's downward cast
  Could make thee somewhat blench or fail,
  Then be my love an idle tale
And fading legend of the past;

And thou, as one that once declined,
  When he was little more than boy,
  On some unworthy heart with joy,
But lives to wed an equal mind,

And breathes a novel world, the while
  His other passion wholly dies,
  Or in the light of deeper eyes
Is matter for a flying smile.

LXIII

Yet pity for a horse o'er-driven,
  And love in which my hound has part,
  Can hang no weight upon my heart
In its assumptions up to heaven;

And I am so much more than these,
  As thou, perchance, art more than I,
  And yet I spare them sympathy,
And I would set their pains at ease.

So mayst thou watch me where I weep,
  As, unto vaster motions bound,
  The circuits of thine orbit round
A higher height, a deeper deep.

LXIV

Dost thou look back on what hath been,
  As some divinely gifted man,
  Whose life in low estate began
And on a simple village green;

Who breaks his birth's invidious bar,
  And grasps the skirts of happy chance,
  And breasts the blows of circumstance,
And grapples with his evil star;

Who makes by force his merit known
  And lives to clutch the golden keys,
  To mould a mighty state's decrees,
And shape the whisper of the throne;

And moving up from high to higher,
  Becomes on Fortune's crowning slope
  The pillar of a people's hope,
The centre of a world's desire;

Yet feels, as in a pensive dream,
  When all his active powers are still,
  A distant dearness in the hill,
A secret sweetness in the stream,

The limit of his narrower fate,
  While yet beside its vocal springs
  He play'd at counsellors and kings,
With one that was his earliest mate;

Who ploughs with pain his native lea
  And reaps the labor of his hands,
  Or in the furrow musing stands:
'Does my old friend remember me?'

LXV

Sweet soul, do with me as thou wilt;
  I lull a fancy trouble-tost
  With 'Love's too precious to be lost
A little grain shall not be spilt.'

And in that solace can I sing,
  Till out of painful phases wrought
  There flutters up a happy thought,
Self-balanced on a lightsome wing;

Since we deserved the name of friends,
  And thine effect so lives in me,
  A part of mine may live in thee
And move thee on to noble ends.

LXVI

You thought my heart too far diseased;
  You wonder when my fancies play
  To find me gay among the gay,
Like one with any trifle pleased.

The shade by which my life was crost,
  Which makes a desert in the mind,
  Has made me kindly with my kind,
And like to him whose sight is lost;

Whose feet are guided thro' the land,
  Whose jest among his friends is free,
  Who takes the children on his knee,
And winds their curls about his hand.

He plays with threads, he beats his chair
  For pastime, dreaming of the sky;
  His inner day can never die,
His night of loss is always there.

LXVII

When on my bed the moonlight falls,
  I know that in thy place of rest
  By that broad water of the west
There comes a glory on the walls:

Thy marble bright in dark appears,
  As slowly steals a silver flame
  Along the letters of thy name,
And o'er the number of thy years.

The mystic glory swims away,
  From off my bed the moonlight dies;
  And closing eaves of wearied eyes
I sleep till dusk is dipt in gray;

And then I know the mist is drawn
  A lucid veil from coast to coast,
  And in the dark church like a ghost
Thy tablet glimmers in the dawn.

LXVIII

When in the down I sink my head,
  Sleep, Death's twin-brother, times my breath;
  Sleep, Death's twin-brother, knows not Death,
Nor can I dream of thee as dead.

I walk as ere I walk'd forlorn,
  When all our path was fresh with dew,
  And all the bugle breezes blew
Reveillée to the breaking morn.

But what is this? I turn about,
  I find a trouble in thine eye,
  Which makes me sad I know not why,
Nor can my dream resolve the doubt;

But ere the lark hath left the lea
 I wake, and I discern the truth;
 It is the trouble of my youth
That foolish sleep transfers to thee.

LXIX

I dream'd there would be Spring no more,
 That Nature's ancient power was lost;
 The streets were black with smoke and frost,
They chatter'd trifles at the door;

I wander'd from the noisy town,
 I found a wood with thorny boughs;
 I took the thorns to bind my brows,
I wore them like a civic crown;

I met with scoffs, I met with scorns
 From youth and babe and hoary hairs:
 They call'd me in the public squares
The fool that wears a crown of thorns.

They call'd me fool, they call'd me child:
 I found an angel of the night;
 The voice was low, the look was bright;
He look'd upon my crown and smiled.

He reach'd the glory of a hand,
 That seem'd to touch it into leaf;
 The voice was not the voice of grief,
The words were hard to understand.

LXX

I cannot see the features right,
　When on the gloom I strive to paint
　The face I know; the hues are faint
And mix with hollow masks of night;

Cloud-towers by ghostly masons wrought,
　A gulf that ever shuts and gapes,
　A hand that points, and palled shapes
In shadowy thoroughfares of thought;

And crowds that stream from yawning doors,
　And shoals of pucker'd faces drive;
　Dark bulks that tumble half alive,
And lazy lengths on boundless shores;

Till all at once beyond the will
　I hear a wizard music roll,
　And thro' a lattice on the soul
Looks thy fair face and makes it still.

LXXI

Sleep, kinsman thou to death and trance
　And madness, thou hast forged at last
　A night-long present of the past
In which we went thro' summer France.

Hadst thou such credit with the soul?
　Then bring an opiate trebly strong,
　Drug down the blindfold sense of wrong,
That so my pleasure may be whole;

While now we talk as once we talk'd
    Of men and minds, the dust of change,
    The days that grow to something strange,
In walking as of old we walk'd

Beside the river's wooded reach,
    The fortress, and the mountain ridge,
    The cataract flashing from the bridge,
The breaker breaking on the beach.

LXXII

Risest thou thus, dim dawn, again,
    And howlest, issuing out of night,
    With blasts that blow the poplar white,
And lash with storm the streaming pane?

Day, when my crown'd estate begun
    To pine in that reverse of doom,
    Which sicken'd every living bloom,
And blurr'd the splendor of the sun;

Who usherest in the dolorous hour
    With thy quick tears that make the rose
    Pull sideways, and the daisy close
Her crimson fringes to the shower;

Who mightst have heaved a windless flame
    Up the deep East, or, whispering, play'd
    A chequer-work of beam and shade
Along the hills, yet look'd the same,

As wan, as chill, as wild as now;
  Day, mark'd as with some hideous crime,
  When the dark hand struck down thro' time,
And cancell'd nature's best: but thou,

Lift as thou mayst thy burthen'd brows
  Thro' clouds that drench the morning star,
  And whirl the ungarner'd sheaf afar,
And sow the sky with flying boughs,

And up thy vault with roaring sound
  Climb thy thick noon, disastrous day;
  Touch thy dull goal of joyless gray,
And hide thy shame beneath the ground.

LXXIII

So many worlds, so much to do,
  So little done, such things to be,
  How know I what had need of thee,
For thou wert strong as thou wert true?

The fame is quench'd that I foresaw,
  The head hath miss'd an earthly wreath:
  I curse not Nature, no, nor Death;
For nothing is that errs from law.

We pass; the path that each man trod
  Is dim, or will be dim, with weeds.
  What fame is left for human deeds
In endless age? It rests with God.

O hollow wraith of dying fame,
　Fade wholly, while the soul exults,
　And self-infolds the large results
Of force that would have forged a name.

LXXIV

As sometimes in a dead man's face,
　To those that watch it more and more,
　A likeness, hardly seen before,
Comes out—to some one of his race;

So, dearest, now thy brows are cold,
　I see thee what thou art, and know
　Thy likeness to the wise below,
Thy kindred with the great of old.

But there is more than I can see,
　And what I see I leave unsaid,
　Nor speak it, knowing Death has made
His darkness beautiful with thee.

LXXV

I leave thy praises unexpress'd
　In verse that brings myself relief,
　And by the measure of my grief
I leave thy greatness to be guess'd.

What practice howsoe'er expert
　In fitting aptest words to things,
　Or voice the richest-toned that sings,
Hath power to give thee as thou wert?

I care not in these fading days
 To raise a cry that lasts not long,
 And round thee with the breeze of song
To stir a little dust of praise.

Thy leaf has perish'd in the green,
 And, while we breathe beneath the sun,
 The world which credits what is done
Is cold to all that might have been.

So here shall silence guard thy fame;
 But somewhere, out of human view,
 Whate'er thy hands are set to do
Is wrought with tumult of acclaim.

LXXVI

Take wings of fancy, and ascend,
 And in a moment set thy face
 Where all the starry heavens of space
Are sharpen'd to a needle's end;

Take wings of foresight; lighten thro'
 The secular abyss to come,
 And lo, thy deepest lays are dumb
Before the mouldering of a yew;

And if the matin songs, that woke
 The darkness of our planet, last,
 Thine own shall wither in the vast,
Ere half the lifetime of an oak.

Ere these have clothed their branchy bowers
  With fifty Mays, thy songs are vain;
  And what are they when these remain
The ruin'd shells of hollow towers?

LXXVII

What hope is here for modern rhyme
  To him who turns a musing eye
  On songs, and deeds, and lives, that lie
Foreshorten'd in the tract of time?

These mortal lullabies of pain
  May bind a book, may line a box,
  May serve to curl a maiden's locks;
Or when a thousand moons shall wane

A man upon a stall may find,
  And, passing, turn the page that tells
  A grief, then changed to something else,
Sung by a long-forgotten mind.

But what of that? My darken'd ways
  Shall ring with music all the same;
  To breathe my loss is more than fame,
To utter love more sweet than praise.

LXXVIII

Again at Christmas did we weave
  The holly round the Christmas hearth;
  The silent snow possess'd the earth,
And calmly fell our Christmas-eve.

The yule-clog sparkled keen with frost,
  No wing of wind the region swept,
  But over all things brooding slept
The quiet sense of something lost.

As in the winters left behind,
  Again our ancient games had place,
  The mimic picture's breathing grace,
And dance and song and hoodman-blind.

Who show'd a token of distress?
  No single tear, no mark of pain—
  O sorrow, then can sorrow wane?
O grief, can grief be changed to less?

O last regret, regret can die!
  No—mixt with all this mystic frame,
  Her deep relations are the same,
But with long use her tears are dry.

LXXIX

'More than my brothers are to me,'—
  Let this not vex thee, noble heart!
  I know thee of what force thou art
To hold the costliest love in fee.

But thou and I are one in kind,
  As moulded like in Nature's mint;
  And hill and wood and field did print
The same sweet forms in either mind.

For us the same cold streamlet curl'd
  Thro' all his eddying coves, the same
  All winds that roam the twilight came
In whispers of the beauteous world.

At one dear knee we proffer'd vows,
  One lesson from one book we learn'd,
  Ere childhood's flaxen ringlet turn'd
To black and brown on kindred brows.

And so my wealth resembles thine,
  But he was rich where I was poor,
  And he supplied my want the more
As his unlikeness fitted mine.

LXXX

If any vague desire should rise,
  That holy Death ere Arthur died
  Had moved me kindly from his side,
And dropt the dust on tearless eyes;

Then fancy shapes, as fancy can,
  The grief my loss in him had wrought,
  A grief as deep as life or thought,
But stay'd in peace with God and man.

I make a picture in the brain;
  I hear the sentence that he speaks;
  He bears the burthen of the weeks,
But turns his burthen into gain.

His credit thus shall set me free;
  And, influence-rich to soothe and save,
  Unused example from the grave
Reach out dead hands to comfort me.

LXXXI

Could I have said while he was here,
  'My love shall now no further range;
  There cannot come a mellower change,
For now is love mature in ear'?

Love, then, had hope of richer store:
  What end is here to my complaint?
  This haunting whisper makes me faint,
'More years had made me love thee more.'

But Death returns an answer sweet:
  'My sudden frost was sudden gain
  And gave all ripeness to the grain,
It might have drawn from after-heat.'

LXXXII

I wage not any feud with Death
  For changes wrought on form and face;
  No lower life that earth's embrace
May breed with him can fright my faith.

Eternal process moving on,
  From state to state the spirit walks;
  And these are but the shatter'd stalks,
Or ruin'd chrysalis of one.

Nor blame I Death, because he bare
  The use of virtue out of earth;
  I know transplanted human worth
Will bloom to profit, otherwhere.

For this alone on Death I wreak
  The wrath that garners in my heart:
  He put our lives so far apart
We cannot hear each other speak.

LXXXIII

Dip down upon the northern shore,
  O sweet new-year delaying long;
  Thou doest expectant Nature wrong;
Delaying long, delay no more.

What stays thee from the clouded noons,
  Thy sweetness from its proper place?
  Can trouble live with April days,
Or sadness in the summer moons?

Bring orchis, bring the foxglove spire,
  The little speedwell's darling blue,
  Deep tulips dash'd with fiery dew,
Laburnums, dropping-wells of fire.

O thou, new-year, delaying long,
  Delayest the sorrow in my blood,
  That longs to burst a frozen bud
And flood a fresher throat with song.

When I contemplate all alone
　　The life that had been thine below,
　　And fix my thoughts on all the glow
To which thy crescent would have grown,

I see thee sitting crown'd with good,
　　A central warmth diffusing bliss
　　In glance and smile, and clasp and kiss,
On all the branches of thy blood;

Thy blood, my friend, and partly mine;
　　For now the day was drawing on,
　　When thou shouldst link thy life with one
Of mine own house, and boys of thine

Had babbled 'Uncle' on my knee;
　　But that remorseless iron hour
　　Made cypress of her orange flower,
Despair of hope, and earth of thee.

I seem to meet their least desire,
　　To clap their cheeks, to call them mine.
　　I see their unborn faces shine
Beside the never-lighted fire.

I see myself an honor'd guest,
　　Thy partner in the flowery walk
　　Of letters, genial table-talk,
Or deep dispute, and graceful jest;

While now thy prosperous labor fills
　The lips of men with honest praise,
　And sun by sun the happy days
Descend below the golden hills

With promise of a morn as fair;
　And all the train of bounteous hours
　Conduct, by paths of growing powers,
To reverence and the silver hair;

Till slowly worn her earthly robe,
　Her lavish mission richly wrought,
　Leaving great legacies of thought,
Thy spirit should fail from off the globe;

What time mine own might also flee,
　As link'd with thine in love and fate,
　And, hovering o'er the dolorous strait
To the other shore, involved in thee,

Arrive at last the blessed goal,
　And He that died in Holy Land
　Would reach us out the shining hand,
And take us as a single soul.

What reed was that on which I leant?
　Ah, backward fancy, wherefore wake
　The old bitterness again, and break
The low beginnings of content!

LXXXV

This truth came borne with bier and pall.
　I felt it, when I sorrow'd most,
　'T is better to have loved and lost,
Than never to have loved at all—

O true in word, and tried in deed,
  Demanding, so to bring relief
  To this which is our common grief,
What kind of life is that I lead;

And whether trust in things above
  Be dimm'd of sorrow, or sustain'd;
  And whether love for him have drain'd
My capabilities of love;

Your words have virtue such as draws
  A faithful answer from the breast,
  Thro' light reproaches, half exprest,
And loyal unto kindly laws.

My blood an even tenor kept,
  Till on mine ear this message falls,
  That in Vienna's fatal walls
God's finger touch'd him, and he slept.

The great Intelligences fair
  That range above our mortal state,
  In circle round the blessed gate,
Received and gave him welcome there;

And led him thro' the blissful climes,
  And show'd him in the fountain fresh
  All knowledge that the sons of flesh
Shall gather in the cycled times.

But I remain'd, whose hopes were dim,
  Whose life, whose thoughts were little worth,
  To wander on a darken'd earth,
Where all things round me breathed of him.

O friendship, equal-poised control,
   O heart, with kindliest motion warm,
   O sacred essence, other form,
O solemn ghost, O crowned soul!

Yet none could better know than I,
   How much of act at human hands
   The sense of human will demands
By which we dare to live or die.

Whatever way my days decline,
   I felt and feel, tho' left alone,
   His being working in mine own,
The footsteps of his life in mine;

A life that all the Muses deck'd
   With gifts of grace, that might express
   All-comprehensive tenderness,
All-subtilizing intellect:

And so my passion hath not swerved
   To works of weakness, but I find
   An image comforting the mind,
And in my grief a strength reserved.

Likewise the imaginative woe,
   That loved to handle spiritual strife,
   Diffused the shock thro' all my life,
But in the present broke the blow.

My pulses therefore beat again
   For other friends that once I met;
   Nor can it suit me to forget
The mighty hopes that make us men.

I woo your love: I count it crime
  To mourn for any overmuch;
  I, the divided half of such
A friendship as had master'd Time;

Which masters Time indeed, and is
  Eternal, separate from fears.
  The all-assuming months and years
Can take no part away from this;

But Summer on the steaming floods,
  And Spring that swells the narrow brooks,
  And Autumn, with a noise of rooks,
That gather in the waning woods,

And every pulse of wind and wave
  Recalls, in change of light or gloom,
  My old affection of the tomb,
And my prime passion in the grave.

My old affection of the tomb,
  A part of stillness, yearns to speak:
  'Arise, and get thee forth and seek
A friendship for the years to come.

'I watch thee from the quiet shore;
  Thy spirit up to mine can reach;
  But in dear words of human speech
We two communicate no more.'

And I, 'Can clouds of nature stain
  The starry clearness of the free?
  How is it? Canst thou feel for me
Some painless sympathy with pain?'

And lightly does the whisper fall:
  ' 'T is hard for thee to fathom this;
  I triumph in conclusive bliss,
And that serene result of all.'

So hold I commerce with the dead;
  Or so methinks the dead would say;
  Or so shall grief with symbols play
And pining life be fancy-fed.

Now looking to some settled end,
  That these things pass, and I shall prove
  A meeting somewhere, love with love,
I crave your pardon, O my friend;

If not so fresh, with love as true,
  I, clasping brother-hands, aver
  I could not, if I would, transfer
The whole I felt for him to you.

For which be they that hold apart
  The promise of the golden hours?
  First love, first friendship, equal powers,
That marry with the virgin heart.

Still mine, that cannot but deplore,
  That beats within a lonely place,
  That yet remembers his embrace,
But at his footstep leaps no more,

My heart, tho' widow'd, may not rest
  Quite in the love of what is gone,
  But seeks to beat in time with one
That warms another living breast.

Ah, take the imperfect gift I bring,
  Knowing the primrose yet is dear,
  The primrose of the later year,
As not unlike to that of Spring.

LXXXVI

Sweet after showers, ambrosial air,
  That rollest from the gorgeous gloom
  Of evening over brake and bloom
And meadow, slowly breathing bare

The round of space, and rapt below
  Thro' all the dewy tassell'd wood,
  And shadowing down the horned flood
In ripples, fan my brows and blow

The fever from my cheek, and sigh
  The full new life that feeds thy breath
  Throughout my frame, till Doubt and Death,
Ill brethren, let the fancy fly

From belt to belt of crimson seas
  On leagues of odor streaming far,
  To where in yonder orient star
A hundred spirits whisper 'Peace.'

LXXXVII

I past beside the reverend walls
  In which of old I wore the gown;
  I roved at random thro' the town,
And saw the tumult of the halls;

And heard once more in college fanes
  The storm their high-built organs make,
  And thunder-music, rolling, shake
The prophet blazon'd on the panes;

And caught once more the distant shout,
  The measured pulse of racing oars
  Among the willows; paced the shores
And many a bridge, and all about

The same gray flats again, and felt
  The same, but not the same; and last
  Up that long walk of limes I past
To see the rooms in which he dwelt.

Another name was on the door.
  I linger'd; all within was noise
  Of songs and clapping hands, and boys
That crash'd the glass and beat the floor;

Where once we held debate, a band
  Of youthful friends, on mind and art,
  And labor, and the changing mart,
And all the framework of the land;

When one would aim an arrow fair,
  But send it slackly from the string;
  And one would pierce an outer ring,
And one an inner, here and there;

And last the master-bowman, he,
  Would cleave the mark. A willing ear
  We lent him. Who but hung to hear
The rapt oration flowing free

From point to point, with power and grace
  And music in the bounds of law,
  To those conclusions when we saw
The God within him light his face,

And seem to lift the form, and glow
  In azure orbits heavenly-wise;
  And over those ethereal eyes
The bar of Michael Angelo?

LXXXVIII

Wild bird, whose warble, liquid sweet,
  Rings Eden thro' the budded quicks,
  O, tell me where the senses mix,
O, tell me where the passions meet,

Whence radiate: fierce extremes employ
  Thy spirits in the darkening leaf,
  And in the midmost heart of grief
Thy passion clasps a secret joy;

And I—my harp would prelude woe—
  I cannot all command the strings;
  The glory of the sum of things
Will flash along the chords and go.

LXXXIX

Witch-elms that counterchange the floor
  Of this flat lawn with dusk and bright;
  And thou, with all thy breadth and height
Of foliage, towering sycamore;

How often, hither wandering down,
  My Arthur found your shadows fair,
  And shook to all the liberal air
The dust and din and steam of town!

He brought an eye for all he saw;
  He mixt in all our simple sports;
  They pleased him, fresh from brawling courts
And dusty purlieus of the law.

O joy to him in this retreat,
  Immantled in ambrosial dark,
  To drink the cooler air, and mark
The landscape winking thro' the heat!

O sound to rout the brood of cares,
  The sweep of scythe in morning dew,
  The gust that round the garden flew,
And tumbled half the mellowing pears!

O bliss, when all in circle drawn
  About him, heart and ear were fed
  To hear him, as he lay and read
The Tuscan poets on the lawn!

Or in the all-golden afternoon
  A guest, or happy sister, sung,
  Or here she brought the harp and flung
A ballad to the brightening moon.

Nor less it pleased in livelier moods,
  Beyond the bounding hill to stray,
  And break the livelong summer day
With banquet in the distant woods;

Whereat we glanced from theme to theme,
  Discuss'd the books to love or hate,
  Or touch'd the changes of the state,
Or threaded some Socratic dream;

But if I praised the busy town,
  He loved to rail against it still,
  For 'ground in yonder social mill
We rub each other's angles down,

'And merge,' he said, 'in form and gloss
  The picturesque of man and man.'
  We talk'd: the stream beneath us ran,
The wine-flask lying couch'd in moss,

Or cool'd within the glooming wave;
  And last, returning from afar,
  Before the crimson-circled star
Had fallen into her father's grave,

And brushing ankle-deep in flowers,
  We heard behind the woodbine veil
  The milk that bubbled in the pail,
And buzzings of the honeyed hours.

XC

He tasted love with half his mind,
  Nor ever drank the inviolate spring
  Where nighest heaven, who first could fling
This bitter seed among mankind:

That could the dead, whose dying eyes
   Were closed with wail, resume their life,
   They would but find in child and wife
An iron welcome when they rise.

'T was well, indeed, when warm with wine,
   To pledge them with a kindly tear,
   To talk them o'er, to wish them here,
To count their memories half divine;

But if they came who past away,
   Behold their brides in other hands:
   The hard heir strides about their lands,
And will not yield them for a day.

Yea, tho' their sons were none of these,
   Not less the yet-loved sire would make
   Confusion worse than death, and shake
The pillars of domestic peace.

Ah, dear, but come thou back to me!
   Whatever change the years have wrought,
   I find not yet one lonely thought
That cries against my wish for thee.

XCI

When rosy plumelets tuft the larch,
   And rarely pipes the mounted thrush,
   Or underneath the barren bush
Flits by the sea-blue bird of March:

Come, wear the form by which I know
  Thy spirit in time among thy peers;
  The hope of unaccomplish'd years
Be large and lucid round thy brow.

When summer's hourly-mellowing change
  May breathe, with many roses sweet,
  Upon the thousand waves of wheat
That ripple round the lowly grange,

Come; not in watches of the night,
  But where the sunbeam broodeth warm,
  Come, beauteous in thine after form,
And like a finer light in light.

XCII

If any vision should reveal
  Thy likeness, I might count it vain
  As but the canker of the brain;
Yea, tho' it spake and made appeal

To chances where our lots were cast
  Together in the days behind,
  I might but say, I hear a wind
Of memory murmuring the past.

Yea, tho' it spake and bared to view
  A fact within the coming year;
  And tho' the months, revolving near,
Should prove the phantom-warning true,

They might not seem thy prophecies,
  But spiritual presentiments,
  And such refraction of events
As often rises ere they rise.

XCIII

I shall not see thee. Dare I say
  No spirit ever brake the band
  That stays him from the native land
Where first he walk'd when claspt in clay?

No visual shade of some one lost,
  But he, the Spirit himself, may come
  Where all the nerve of sense is numb,
Spirit to Spirit, Ghost to Ghost.

O, therefore from thy sightless range
  With gods in unconjectured bliss,
  O, from the distance of the abyss
Of tenfold-complicated change,

Descend, and touch, and enter; hear
  The wish too strong for words to name,
  That in this blindness of the frame
My Ghost may feel that thine is near.

XCIV

How pure at heart and sound in head,
  With what divine affections bold
  Should be the man whose thought would hold
An hour's communion with the dead.

In vain shalt thou, or any, call
  The spirits from their golden day,
  Except, like them, thou too canst say,
My spirit is at peace with all.

They haunt the silence of the breast,
  Imaginations calm and fair,
  The memory like a cloudless air,
The conscience as a sea at rest;

But when the heart is full of din,
  And doubt beside the portal waits,
  They can but listen at the gates,
And hear the household jar within.

XCV

By night we linger'd on the lawn,
  For underfoot the herb was dry;
  And genial warmth; and o'er the sky
The silvery haze of summer drawn;

And calm that let the tapers burn
  Unwavering: not a cricket chirr'd;
  The brook alone far-off was heard,
And on the board the fluttering urn.

And bats went round in fragrant skies,
  And wheel'd or lit the filmy shapes
  That haunt the dusk, with ermine capes
And woolly breasts and beaded eyes;

While now we sang old songs that peal'd
  From knoll to knoll, where, couch'd at ease,
  The white kine glimmer'd, and the trees
Laid their dark arms about the field.

But when those others, one by one,
  Withdrew themselves from me and night,
  And in the house light after light
Went out, and I was all alone,

A hunger seized my heart; I read
  Of that glad year which once had been,
  In those fallen leaves which kept their green,
The noble letters of the dead.

And strangely on the silence broke
  The silent-speaking words, and strange
  Was love's dumb cry defying change
To test his worth; and strangely spoke

The faith, the vigor, bold to dwell
  On doubts that drive the coward back,
  And keen thro' wordy snares to track
Suggestion to her inmost cell.

So word by word, and line by line,
  The dead man touch'd me from the past,
  And all at once it seem'd at last
The living soul was flash'd on mine,

And mine in this was wound, and whirl'd
  About empyreal heights of thought,
  And came on that which is, and caught
The deep pulsations of the world,

Æonian music measuring out
   The steps of Time—the shocks of Chance—
   The blows of Death. At length my trance
Was cancell'd, stricken thro' with doubt.

Vague words! but ah, how hard to frame
   In matter-moulded forms of speech,
   Or even for intellect to reach
Thro' memory that which I became;

Till now the doubtful dusk reveal'd
   The knolls once more where, couch'd at ease,
   The white kine glimmer'd, and the trees
Laid their dark arms about the field;

And suck'd from out the distant gloom
   A breeze began to tremble o'er
   The large leaves of the sycamore,
And fluctuate all the still perfume,

And gathering freshlier overhead,
   Rock'd the full-foliaged elms, and swung
   The heavy-folded rose, and flung
The lilies to and fro, and said,

'The dawn, the dawn,' and died away;
   And East and West, without a breath,
   Mixt their dim lights, like life and death,
To broaden into boundless day.

XCVI

You say, but with no touch of scorn,
   Sweet-hearted, you, whose light-blue eyes
   Are tender over drowning flies,
You tell me, doubt is Devil-born.

I know not: one indeed I knew
    In many a subtle question versed,
    Who touch'd a jarring lyre at first,
But ever strove to make it true;

Perplext in faith, but pure in deeds,
    At last he beat his music out.
    There lives more faith in honest doubt,
Believe me, than in half the creeds.

He fought his doubts and gather'd strength,
    He would not make his judgment blind,
    He faced the spectres of the mind
And laid them; thus he came at length

To find a stronger faith his own,
    And Power was with him in the night,
    Which makes the darkness and the light,
And dwells not in the light alone,

But in the darkness and the cloud,
    As over Sinaï's peaks of old,
    While Israel made their gods of gold,
Altho' the trumpet blew so loud.

XCVII

My love has talk'd with rocks and trees;
    He finds on misty mountain-ground
    His own vast shadow glory-crown'd;
He sees himself in all he sees.

Two partners of a married life—
   I look'd on these and thought of thee
   In vastness and in mystery,
And of my spirit as of a wife.

These two—they dwelt with eye on eye,
   Their hearts of old have beat in tune,
   Their meetings made December June,
Their every parting was to die.

Their love has never past away;
   The days she never can forget
   Are earnest that he loves her yet,
Whate'er the faithless people say.

Her life is lone, he sits apart;
   He loves her yet, she will not weep,
   Tho' rapt in matters dark and deep
He seems to slight her simple heart.

He thrids the labyrinth of the mind,
   He reads the secret of the star,
   He seems so near and yet so far,
He looks so cold: she thinks him kind.

She keeps the gift of years before,
   A wither'd violet is her bliss;
   She knows not what his greatness is,
For that, for all, she loves him more.

For him she plays, to him she sings
   Of early faith and plighted vows;
   She knows but matters of the house,
And he, he knows a thousand things.

Her faith is fixt and cannot move,
  She darkly feels him great and wise
  She dwells on him with faithful eyes
'I cannot understand; I love.'

XCVIII

You leave us: you will see the Rhine,
  And those fair hills I sail'd below,
  When I was there with him; and go
By summer belts of wheat and vine

To where he breathed his latest breath,
  That city. All her splendor seems
  No livelier than the wisp that gleams
On Lethe in the eyes of Death.

Let her great Danube rolling fair
  Enwind her isles, unmark'd of me;
  I have not seen, I will not see
Vienna; rather dream that there,

A treble darkness, Evil haunts
  The birth, the bridal; friend from friend
  Is oftener parted, fathers bend
Above more graves, a thousand wants

Gnarr at the heels of men, and prey
  By each cold hearth, and sadness flings
  Her shadow on the blaze of kings.
And yet myself have heard him say,

That not in any mother town
　　With statelier progress to and fro
　　The double tides of chariots flow
By park and suburb under brown

Of lustier leaves; nor more content,
　　He told me, lives in any crowd,
　　When all is gay with lamps, and loud
With sport and song, in booth and tent.

Imperial halls, or open plain;
　　And wheels the circled dance, and breaks
　　The rocket molten into flakes
Of crimson or in emerald rain.

XCIX

Risest thou thus, dim dawn, again,
　　So loud with voices of the birds,
　　So thick with lowings of the herds,
Day, when I lost the flower of men;

Who tremblest thro' thy darkling red
　　On yon swollen brook that bubbles fast
　　By meadows breathing of the past,
And woodlands holy to the dead;

Who murmurest in the foliaged eaves
　　A song that slights the coming care,
　　And Autumn laying here and there
A fiery finger on the leaves;

Who wakenest with thy balmy breath
  To myriads on the genial earth,
  Memories of bridal, or of birth,
And unto myriads more, of death.

O, wheresoever those may be,
  Betwixt the slumber of the poles,
  To-day they count as kindred souls;
They know me not, but mourn with me.

C

I climb the hill: from end to end
  Of all the landscape underneath,
  I find no place that does not breathe
Some gracious memory of my friend;

No gray old grange, or lonely fold,
  Or low morass and whispering reed,
  Or simple stile from mead to mead,
Or sheepwalk up the windy wold;

Nor hoary knoll of ash and haw
  That hears the latest linnet trill,
  Nor quarry trench'd along the hill
And haunted by the wrangling daw;

Nor runlet tinkling from the rock;
  Nor pastoral rivulet that swerves
  To left and right thro' meadowy curves,
That feed the mothers of the flock;

But each has pleased a kindred eye,
  And each reflects a kindlier day;
  And, leaving these, to pass away,
I think once more he seems to die.

CI

Unwatch'd, the garden bough shall sway,
  The tender blossom flutter down,
  Unloved, that beech will gather brown,
This maple burn itself away;

Unloved, the sunflower, shining fair,
  Ray round with flames her disk of seed,
  And many a rose-carnation feed
With summer spice the humming air;

Unloved, by many a sandy bar,
  The brook shall babble down the plain,
  At noon or when the Lesser Wain
Is twisting round the polar star;

Uncared for, gird the windy grove,
  And flood the haunts of hern and crake,
  Or into silver arrows break
The sailing moon in creek and cove;

Till from the garden and the wild
  A fresh association blow,
  And year by year the landscape grow
Familiar to the stranger's child;

As year by year the laborer tills
  His wonted glebe, or lops the glades,
  And year by year our memory fades
From all the circle of the hills.

CII

We leave the well-beloved place
  Where first we gazed upon the sky;
  The roofs that heard our earliest cry
Will shelter one of stranger race.

We go, but ere we go from home,
  As down the garden-walks I move,
  Two spirits of a diverse love
Contend for loving masterdom.

One whispers, 'Here thy boyhood sung
  Long since its matin song, and heard
  The low love-language of the bird
In native hazels tassel-hung.'

The other answers, 'Yea, but here
  Thy feet have stray'd in after hours
  With thy lost friend among the bowers,
And this hath made them trebly dear.'

These two have striven half the day,
  And each prefers his separate claim,
  Poor rivals in a losing game,
That will not yield each other way.

I turn to go; my feet are set
  To leave the pleasant fields and farms;
  They mix in one another's arms
To one pure image of regret.

CIII

On that last night before we went
  From out the doors where I was bred,
  I dream'd a vision of the dead,
Which left my after-morn content.

Methought I dwelt within a hall,
  And maidens with me; distant hills
  From hidden summits fed with rills
A river sliding by the wall.

The hall with harp and carol rang.
  They sang of what is wise and good
  And graceful. In the centre stood
A statue veil'd, to which they sang;

And which, tho' veil'd, was known to me,
  The shape of him I loved, and love
  For ever. Then flew in a dove
And brought a summons from the sea;

And when they learnt that I must go,
  They wept and wail'd, but led the way
  To where a little shallop lay
At anchor in the flood below;

And on by many a level mead,
  And shadowing bluff that made the banks,
  We glided winding under ranks
Of iris and the golden reed;

And still as vaster grew the shore
   And roll'd the floods in grander space,
   The maidens gather'd strength and grace
And presence, lordlier than before;

And I myself, who sat apart
   And watch'd them, wax'd in every limb;
   I felt the thews of Anakim,
The pulses of a Titan's heart;

As one would sing the death of war,
   And one would chant the history
   Of that great race which is to be,
And one the shaping of a star;

Until the forward-creeping tides
   Began to foam, and we to draw
   From deep to deep, to where we saw
A great ship lift her shining sides.

The man we loved was there on deck,
   But thrice as large as man he bent
   To greet us. Up the side I went,
And fell in silence on his neck;

Whereat those maidens with one mind
   Bewail'd their lot; I did them wrong:
   'We served thee here,' they said, 'so long,
And wilt thou leave us now behind?'

So rapt I was, they could not win
   An answer from my lips, but he
   Replying, 'Enter likewise ye
And go with us:' they enter'd in.

And while the wind began to sweep
   A music out of sheet and shroud,
   We steer'd her toward a crimson cloud
That landlike slept along the deep.

CIV

The time draws near the birth of Christ;
   The moon is hid, the night is still;
   A single church below the hill
Is pealing, folded in the mist.

A single peal of bells below,
   That wakens at this hour of rest
   A single murmur in the breast,
That these are not the bells I know.

Like strangers' voices here they sound,
   In lands where not a memory strays,
   Nor landmark breathes of other days,
But all is new unhallow'd ground.

CV

To-night ungather'd let us leave
   This laurel, let this holly stand:
   We live within the stranger's land,
And strangely falls our Christmas-eve.

Our father's dust is left alone
   And silent under other snows:
   There in due time the woodbine blows,
The violet comes, but we are gone.

No more shall wayward grief abuse
 The genial hour with mask and mime;
 For change of place, like growth of time,
Has broke the bond of dying use.

Let cares that petty shadows cast,
 By which our lives are chiefly proved,
 A little spare the night I loved,
And hold it solemn to the past.

But let no footstep beat the floor,
 Nor bowl of wassail mantle warm;
 For who would keep an ancient form
Thro' which the spirit breathes no more?

Be neither song, nor game, nor feast;
 Nor harp be touch'd, nor flute be blown;
 No dance, no motion, save alone
What lightens in the lucid East

Of rising worlds by yonder wood.
 Long sleeps the summer in the seed;
 Run out your measured arcs, and lead
The closing cycle rich in good.

CVI

Ring out, wild bells, to the wild sky,
 The flying cloud, the frosty light:
 The year is dying in the night;
Ring out, wild bells, and let him die.

Ring out the old, ring in the new,
  Ring, happy bells, across the snow;
  The year is going, let him go;
Ring out the false, ring in the true.

Ring out the grief that saps the mind,
  For those that here we see no more;
  Ring out the feud of rich and poor,
Ring in redress to all mankind.

Ring out a slowly dying cause,
  And ancient forms of party strife;
  Ring in the nobler modes of life,
With sweeter manners, purer laws.

Ring out the want, the care, the sin,
  The faithless coldness of the times;
  Ring out, ring out my mournful rhymes,
But ring the fuller minstrel in.

Ring out false pride in place and blood,
  The civic slander and the spite;
  Ring in the love of truth and right,
Ring in the common love of good.

Ring out old shapes of foul disease;
  Ring out the narrowing lust of gold;
  Ring out the thousand wars of old,
Ring in the thousand years of peace.

Ring in the valiant man and free,
  The larger heart, the kindlier hand;
  Ring out the darkness of the land,
Ring in the Christ that is to be.

It is the day when he was born,
  A bitter day that early sank
  Behind a purple-frosty bank
Of vapor, leaving night forlorn.

The time admits not flowers or leaves
  To deck the banquet. Fiercely flies
  The blast of North and East, and ice
Makes daggers at the sharpen'd eaves,

And bristles all the brakes and thorns
  To yon hard crescent, as she hangs
  Above the wood which grides and clangs
Its leafless ribs and iron horns

Together, in the drifts that pass
  To darken on the rolling brine
  That breaks the coast. But fetch the wine,
Arrange the board and brim the glass;

Bring in great logs and let them lie,
  To make a solid core of heat;
  Be cheerful-minded, talk and treat
Of all things even as he were by;

We keep the day. With festal cheer,
  With books and music, surely we
  Will drink to him, whate'er he be,
And sing the songs he loved to hear.

CVIII

I will not shut me from my kind,
  And, lest I stiffen into stone,
  I will not eat my heart alone,
Nor feed with sighs a passing wind:

What profit lies in barren faith,
  And vacant yearning, tho' with might
  To scale the heaven's highest height,
Or dive below the wells of death?

What find I in the highest place,
  But mine own phantom chanting hymns?
  And on the depths of death there swims
The reflex of a human face.

I 'll rather take what fruit may be
  Of sorrow under human skies:
  'T is held that sorrow makes us wise,
Whatever wisdom sleep with thee.

CIX

Heart-affluence in discursive talk
  From household fountains never dry;
  The critic clearness of an eye
That saw thro' all the Muses' walk;

Seraphic intellect and force
  To seize and throw the doubts of man;
  Impassion'd logic, which outran
The hearer in its fiery course;

High nature amorous of the good,
  But touch'd with no ascetic gloom;
  And passion pure in snowy bloom
Thro' all the years of April blood;

A love of freedom rarely felt,
  Of freedom in her regal seat
  Of England; not the schoolboy heat,
The blind hysterics of the Celt;

And manhood fused with female grace
  In such a sort, the child would twine
  A trustful hand, unask'd, in thine,
And find his comfort in thy face;

All these have been, and thee mine eyes
  Have look'd on: if they look'd in vain,
  My shame is greater who remain,
Nor let thy wisdom make me wise.

CX

Thy converse drew us with delight,
  The men of rathe and riper years;
  The feeble soul, a haunt of fears,
Forgot his weakness in thy sight.

On thee the loyal-hearted hung,
  The proud was half disarm'd of pride,
  Nor cared the serpent at thy side
To flicker with his double tongue.

The stern were mild when thou wert by,
　The flippant put himself to school
　And heard thee, and the brazen fool
Was soften'd, and he knew not why;

While I, thy nearest, sat apart,
　And felt thy triumph was as mine;
　And loved them more, that they were thine,
The graceful tact, the Christian art;

Nor mine the sweetness or the skill,
　But mine the love that will not tire,
　And, born of love, the vague desire
That spurs an imitative will.

CXI

The churl in spirit, up or down
　Along the scale of ranks, thro' all,
　To him who grasps a golden ball,
By blood a king, at heart a clown,—

The churl in spirit, howe'er he veil
　His want in forms for fashion's sake,
　Will let his coltish nature break
At seasons thro' the gilded pale;

For who can always act? but he,
　To whom a thousand memories call,
　Not being less but more than all
The gentleness he seem'd to be,

Best seem'd the thing he was, and join'd
　　Each office of the social hour
　　To noble manners, as the flower
And native growth of noble mind;

Nor ever narrowness or spite,
　　Or villain fancy fleeting by,
　　Drew in the expression of an eye
Where God and Nature met in light;

And thus he bore without abuse
　　The grand old name of gentleman,
　　Defamed by every charlatan,
And soil'd with all ignoble use.

CXII

High wisdom holds my wisdom less,
　　That I, who gaze with temperate eyes
　　On glorious insufficiencies,
Set light by narrower perfectness.

But thou, that fillest all the room
　　Of all my love, art reason why
　　I seem to cast a careless eye
On souls, the lesser lords of doom.

For what wert thou? some novel power
　　Sprang up for ever at a touch,
　　And hope could never hope too much,
In watching thee from hour to hour,

Large elements in order brought,
　　And tracts of calm from tempest made,
　　And world-wide fluctuation sway'd
In vassal tides that follow'd thought.

CXIII

'T is held that sorrow makes us wise;
　　Yet how much wisdom sleeps with thee
　　Which not alone had guided me,
But served the seasons that may rise;

For can I doubt, who knew thee keen
　　In intellect, with force and skill
　　To strive, to fashion, to fulfil—
I doubt not what thou wouldst have been:

A life in civic action warm,
　　A soul on highest mission sent,
　　A potent voice of Parliament,
A pillar steadfast in the storm,

Should licensed boldness gather force,
　　Becoming, when the time has birth,
　　A lever to uplift the earth
And roll it in another course,

With thousand shocks that come and go,
　　With agonies, with energies,
　　With overthrowings, and with cries,
And undulations to and fro.

Who loves not Knowledge? Who shall rail
   Against her beauty? May she mix
   With men and prosper! Who shall fix
Her pillars? Let her work prevail.

But on her forehead sits a fire;
   She sets her forward countenance
   And leaps into the future chance,
Submitting all things to desire.

Half-grown as yet, a child, and vain—
   She cannot fight the fear of death.
   What is she, cut from love and faith,
But some wild Pallas from the brain

Of demons? fiery-hot to burst
   All barriers in her onward race
   For power. Let her know her place;
She is the second, not the first.

A higher hand must make her mild,
   If all be not in vain, and guide
   Her footsteps, moving side by side
With Wisdom, like the younger child;

For she is earthly of the mind,
   But Wisdom heavenly of the soul.
   O friend, who camest to thy goal
So early, leaving me behind,

I would the great world grew like thee,
  Who grewest not alone in power
  And knowledge, but by year and hour
In reverence and in charity.

CXV

Now fades the last long streak of snow,
  Now burgeons every maze of quick
  About the flowering squares, and thick
By ashen roots the violets blow.

Now rings the woodland loud and long,
  The distance takes a lovelier hue,
  And drown'd in yonder living blue
The lark becomes a sightless song.

Now dance the lights on lawn and lea,
  The flocks are whiter down the vale,
  And milkier every milky sail
On winding stream or distant sea;

Where now the seamew pipes, or dives
  In yonder greening gleam, and fly
  The happy birds, that change their sky
To build and brood, that live their lives

From land to land; and in my breast
  Spring wakens too, and my regret
  Becomes an April violet,
And buds and blossoms like the rest.

CXVI

Is it, then, regret for buried time
    That keenlier in sweet April wakes,
    And meets the year, and gives and takes
The colors of the crescent prime?

Not all; the songs, the stirring air,
    The life re-orient out of dust,
    Cry thro' the sense to hearten trust
In that which made the world so fair.

Not all regret: the face will shine
    Upon me, while I muse alone,
    And that dear voice, I once have known,
Still speak to me of me and mine.

Yet less of sorrow lives in me
    For days of happy commune dead,
    Less yearning for the friendship fled
Than some strong bond which is to be.

CXVII

O days and hours, your work is this,
    To hold me from my proper place,
    A little while from his embrace,
For fuller gain of after bliss;

That out of distance might ensue
    Desire of nearness doubly sweet,
    And unto meeting, when we meet,
Delight a hundredfold accrue,

For every grain of sand that runs,
  And every span of shade that steals,
  And every kiss of toothed wheels,
And all the courses of the suns.

CXVIII

Contemplate all this work of Time,
  The giant laboring in his youth;
  Nor dream of human love and truth,
As dying Nature's earth and lime;

But trust that those we call the dead
  Are breathers of an ampler day
  For ever nobler ends. They say,
The solid earth whereon we tread

In tracts of fluent heat began,
  And grew to seeming-random forms,
  The seeming prey of cyclic storms,
Till at the last arose the man;

Who throve and branch'd from clime to clime,
  The herald of a higher race,
  And of himself in higher place,
If so he type this work of time

Within himself, from more to more;
  Or, crown'd with attributes of woe
  Like glories, move his course, and show
That life is not as idle ore,

But iron dug from central gloom,
   And heated hot with burning fears,
   And dipt in baths of hissing tears,
And batter'd with the shocks of doom

To shape and use. Arise and fly
   The reeling Faun, the sensual feast;
   Move upward, working out the beast,
And let the ape and tiger die.

CXIX

Doors, where my heart was used to beat
   So quickly, not as one that weeps
   I come once more; the city sleeps;
I smell the meadow in the street;

I hear a chirp of birds; I see
   Betwixt the black fronts long-with-drawn
   A light-blue lane of early dawn,
And think of early days and thee,

And bless thee, for thy lips are bland,
   And bright the friendship of thine eye;
   And in my thoughts with scarce a sigh
I take the pressure of thine hand.

CXX

I trust I have not wasted breath:
   I think we are not wholly brain,
   Magnetic mockeries; not in vain,
Like Paul with beasts, I fought with Death;

Not only cunning casts in clay:
    Let Science prove we are, and then
    What matters Science unto men,
At least to me? I would not stay.

Let him, the wiser man who springs
    Hereafter, up from childhood shape
    His action like the greater ape,
But I was *born* to other things.

CXXI

Sad Hesper o'er the buried sun
    And ready, thou, to die with him,
    Thou watchest all things ever dim
An dimmer, and a glory done.

The team is loosen'd from the wain,
    The boat is drawn upon the shore;
    Thou listenest to the closing door,
And life is darken'd in the brain.

Bright Phosphor, fresher for the night,
    By thee the world's great work is heard
    Beginning, and the wakeful bird;
Behind thee comes the greater light.

The market boat is on the stream,
    And voices hail it from the brink;
    Thou hear'st the village hammer clink,
And see'st the moving of the team.

Sweet Hesper-Phosphor, double name
    For what is one, the first, the last,
    Thou, like my present and my past,
Thy place is changed; thou art the same.

CXXII

O, wast thou with me, dearest, then,
  While I rose up against my doom,
  And yearn'd to burst the folded gloom,
To bare the eternal heavens again,

To feel once more, in placid awe,
  The strong imagination roll
  A sphere of stars about my soul,
In all her motion one with law?

If thou wert with me, and the grave
  Divide us not, be with me now,
  And enter in at breast and brow,
Till all my blood, a fuller wave,

Be quicken'd with a livelier breath,
  And like an inconsiderate boy,
  As in the former flash of joy,
I slip the thoughts of life and death;

And all the breeze of Fancy blows,
  And every dewdrop paints a bow,
  The wizard lightnings deeply glow,
And every thought breaks out a rose.

CXXIII

There rolls the deep where grew the tree.
  O earth, what changes hast thou seen!
  There where the long street roars hath been
The stillness of the central sea.

The hills are shadows, and they flow
  From form to form, and nothing stands;
  They melt like mist, the solid lands,
Like clouds they shape themselves and go.

But in my spirit will I dwell,
  And dream my dream, and hold it true;
  For tho' my lips may breathe adieu,
I cannot think the thing farewell.

CXXIV

That which we dare invoke to bless;
  Our dearest faith; our ghastliest doubt;
  He, They, One, All; within, without;
The Power in darkness whom we guess,—

I found Him not in world or sun,
  Or eagle's wing, or insect's eye,
  Nor thro' the questions men may try,
The petty cobwebs we have spun.

If e'er when faith had fallen asleep,
  I heard a voice, 'believe no more,'
  And heard an ever-breaking shore
That tumbled in the Godless deep,

A warmth within the breast would melt
  The freezing reason's colder part,
  And like a man in wrath the heart
Stood up and answer'd, 'I have felt.'

No, like a child in doubt and fear:
  But that blind clamor made me wise;
  Then was I as a child that cries,
But, crying, knows his father near;

And what I am beheld again
 What is, and no man understands;
 And out of darkness came the hands
That reach thro' nature, moulding men.

CXXV

Whatever I have said or sung,
 Some bitter notes my harp would give,
 Yea, tho' there often seem'd to live
A contradiction on the tongue,

Yet Hope had never lost her youth,
 She did but look through dimmer eyes;
 Or Love but play'd with gracious lies,
Because he felt so fix'd in truth;

And if the song were full of care,
 He breathed the spirit of the song;
 And if the words were sweet and strong
He set his royal signet there;

Abiding with me till I sail
 To seek thee on the mystic deeps,
 And this electric force, that keeps
A thousand pulses dancing, fail.

CXXVI

Love is and was my lord and king,
 And in his presence I attend
 To hear the tidings of my friend,
Which every hour his couriers bring.

Love is and was my king and lord,
　And will be, tho' as yet I keep
　Within the court on earth, and sleep
Encompass'd by his faithful guard,

And hear at times a sentinel
　Who moves about from place to place,
　And whispers to the worlds of space,
In the deep night, that all is well.

CXXVII

And all is well, tho' faith and form
　Be sunder'd in the night of fear;
　Well roars the storm to those that hear
A deeper voice across the storm,

Proclaiming social truth shall spread,
　And justice, even tho' thrice again
　The red fool-fury of the Seine
Should pile her barricades with dead.

But ill for him that wears a crown,
　And him, the lazar, in his rags!
　They tremble, the sustaining crags;
The spires of ice are toppled down,

And molten up, and roar in flood;
　The fortress crashes from on high,
　The brute earth lightens to the sky
And the great Æon sinks in blood,

And compass'd by the fires of hell;
　While thou, dear spirit, happy star,

O'erlook'st the tumult from afar,
And smilest, knowing all is well.

CXXVIII

The love that rose on stronger wings,
  Unpalsied when he met with Death,
  Is comrade of the lesser faith
That sees the course of human things.

No doubt vast eddies in the flood
  Of onward time shall yet be made,
  And throned races may degrade;
Yet, O ye mysteries of good,

Wild Hours that fly with Hope and Fear,
  If all your office had to do
  With old results that look like new—
If this were all your mission here,

To draw, to sheathe a useless sword,
  To fool the crowd with glorious lies,
  To cleave a creed in sects and cries,
To change the bearing of a word,

To shift an arbitrary power,
  To cramp the student at his desk,
  To make old bareness picturesque
And tuft with grass a feudal tower,

Why, then my scorn might well descend
  On you and yours. I see in part
  That all, as in some piece of art,
Is toil coöperant to an end.

CXXIX

Dear friend, far off, my lost desire,
  So far, so near in woe and weal,
  O loved the most, when most I feel
There is a lower and a higher;

Known and unknown, human, divine;
  Sweet human hand and lips and eye;
  Dear heavenly friend that canst not die,
Mine, mine, for ever, ever mine;

Strange friend, past, present, and to be;
  Loved deeplier, darklier understood;
  Behold, I dream a dream of good,
And mingle all the world with thee.

CXXX

Thy voice is on the rolling air;
  I hear thee where the waters run;
  Thou standest in the rising sun,
And in the setting thou art fair.

What art thou then? I cannot guess;
  But tho' I seem in star and flower
  To feel thee some diffusive power,
I do not therefore love thee less.

My love involves the love before;
  My love is vaster passion now;
  Tho' mix'd with God and Nature thou,
I seem to love thee more and more.

Far off thou art, but ever nigh;
  I have thee still, and I rejoice;
  I prosper, circled with thy voice;
I shall not lose thee tho' I die.

CXXXI

O living will that shalt endure
  When all that seems shall suffer shock,
  Rise in the spiritual rock,
Flow thro' our deeds and make them pure,

That we may lift from out of dust
  A voice as unto him that hears,
  A cry above the conquer'd years
To one that with us works, and trust,

With faith that comes of self-control,
  The truths that never can be proved
  Until we close with all we loved,
And all we flow from, soul in soul.

———

O true and tried, so well and long,
  Demand not thou a marriage lay;
  In that it is thy marriage day
Is music more than any song.

Nor have I felt so much of bliss
  Since first he told me that he loved
  A daughter of our house, nor proved
Since that dark day a day like this;

Tho' I since then have number'd o'er
  Some thrice three years; they went and came,
  Remade the blood and changed the frame,
And yet is love not less, but more;

No longer caring to embalm
  In dying songs a dead regret,
  But like a statue solid-set,
And moulded in colossal calm.

Regret is dead, but love is more
  Than in the summers that are flown,
  For I myself with these have grown
To something greater than before;

Which makes appear the songs I made
  As echoes out of weaker times,
  As half but idle brawling rhymes,
The sport of random sun and shade.

But where is she, the bridal flower,
  That must be made a wife ere noon?
  She enters, glowing like the moon
Of Eden on its bridal bower.

On me she bends her blissful eyes
  And then on thee; they meet thy look
  And brighten like the star that shook
Betwixt the palms of Paradise.

O, when her life was yet in bud,
  He too foretold the perfect rose.
  For thee she grew, for thee she grows
For ever, and as fair as good.

And thou art worthy, full of power;
　As gentle; liberal-minded, great,
　Consistent; wearing all that weight
Of learning lightly like a flower.

But now set out: the noon is near,
　And I must give away the bride;
　She fears not, or with thee beside
And me behind her, will not fear.

For I that danced her on my knee,
　That watch'd her on her nurse's arm,
　That shielded all her life from harm,
At last must part with her to thee;

Now waiting to be made a wife,
　Her feet, my darling, on the dead;
　Their pensive tablets round her head,
And the most living words of life

Breathed in her ear. The ring is on,
　The 'Wilt thou?' answer'd, and again
　The 'Wilt thou?' ask'd, till out of twain
Her sweet 'I will' has made you one.

Now sign your names, which shall be read,
　Mute symbols of a joyful morn,
　By village eyes as yet unborn.
The names are sign'd, and overhead

Begins the clash and clang that tells
　The joy to every wandering breeze;
　The blind wall rocks, and on the trees
The dead leaf trembles to the bells.

O happy hour, and happier hours
　　Await them.　Many a merry face
　　Salutes them—maidens of the place,
That pelt us in the porch with flowers.

O happy hour, behold the bride
　　With him to whom her hand I gave.
　　They leave the porch, they pass the grave
That has to-day its sunny side.

To-day the grave is bright for me,
　　For them the light of life increased,
　　Who stay to share the morning feast,
Who rest to-night beside the sea.

Let all my genial spirits advance
　　To meet and greet a whiter sun;
　　My drooping memory will not shun
The foaming grape of eastern France.

It circles round, and fancy plays,
　　And hearts are warm'd and faces bloom,
　　As drinking health to bride and groom
We wish them store of happy days.

Nor count me all to blame if I
　　Conjecture of a stiller guest,
　　Perchance, perchance, among the rest,
And, tho' in silence, wishing joy.

But they must go, the time draws on,
　　And those white-favor'd horses wait;
　　They rise, but linger; it is late;
Farewell, we kiss, and they are gone.

A shade falls on us like the dark
  From little cloudlets on the grass,
  But sweeps away as out we pass
To range the woods, to roam the park,

Discussing how their courtship grew,
  And talk of others that are wed,
  And how she look'd, and what he said,
And back we come at fall of dew.

Again the feast, the speech, the glee,
  The shade of passing thought, the wealth
  Of words and wit, the double health,
The crowning cup, the three-times-three,

And last the dance;—till I retire.
  Dumb is that tower which spake so loud,
  And high in heaven the streaming cloud,
And on the downs a rising fire:

And rise, O moon, from yonder down,
  Till over down and over dale
  All night the shining vapor sail
And pass the silent-lighted town,

The white-faced halls, the glancing rills,
  And catch at every mountain head,
  And o'er the friths that branch and spread
Their sleeping silver thro' the hills;

And touch with shade the bridal doors,
  With tender gloom the roof, the wall;
  And breaking let the splendor fall
To spangle all the happy shores

By which they rest, and ocean sounds,
  And, star and system rolling past,
  A soul shall draw from out the vast
And strike his being into bounds,

And, moved thro' life of lower phase,
  Result in man, be born and think,
  And act and love, a closer link
Betwixt us and the crowning race

Of those that, eye to eye, shall look
  On knowledge; under whose command
  Is Earth and Earth's, and in their hand
Is Nature like an open book;

No longer half-akin to brute,
  For all we thought and loved and did,
  And hoped, and suffer'd, is but seed
Of what in them is flower and fruit;

Whereof the man that with me trod
  This planet was a noble type
  Appearing ere the times were ripe,
That friend of mine who lives in God,

That God, which ever lives and loves,
  One God, one law, one element,
  And one far-off divine event,
To which the whole creation moves.

PRO PATRIA

THE REVENGE

A BALLAD OF THE FLEET

AT FLORES in the Azores Sir Richard Grenville lay,
And a pinnace, like a flutter'd bird, came flying from far away;
'Spanish ships of war at sea! we have sighted fifty-three!'
Then sware Lord Thomas Howard: ' 'Fore God I am no
    coward;
But I cannot meet them here, for my ships are out of gear,
And the half my men are sick. I must fly, but follow quick.
We are six ships of the line; can we fight with fifty-three?'

Then spake Sir Richard Grenville: 'I know you are no coward;
You fly them for a moment to fight with them again.
But I 've ninety men and more that are lying sick ashore.
I should count myself the coward if I left them, my Lord
    Howard,
To these Inquisition dogs and the devildoms of Spain.'

So Lord Howard past away with five ships of war that day,
Till he melted like a cloud in the silent summer heaven;
But Sir Richard bore in hand all his sick men from the land
Very carefully and slow,
Men of Bideford in Devon,
And we laid them on the ballast down below;
For we brought them all aboard,
And they blest him in their pain, that they were not left to
    Spain,
To the thumb-screw and the stake, for the glory of the Lord.

He had only a hundred seamen to work the ship and to fight,
And he sailed away from Flores till the Spaniard came in
    sight,
With his huge sea-castles heaving upon the weather bow.
'Shall we fight or shall we fly?
Good Sir Richard, tell us now,
For to fight is but to die!
There 'll be little of us left by the time this sun be set.'
And Sir Richard said again: 'We be all good English men.
Let us bang these dogs of Seville, the children of the devil,
I never turn'd my back upon Don or devil yet.'

Sir Richard spoke and he laugh'd, and we roar'd a hurrah,
    and so
The little Revenge ran on sheer into the heart of the foe,
With her hundred fighters on deck, and her ninety sick below;
For half of their fleet to the right and half to the left were
    seen,
And the little Revenge ran on thro' the long sea-lane between.

Thousands of their soldiers look'd down from their decks and
    laugh'd,
Thousands of their seamen made mock at the mad little craft
Running on and on, till delay'd
By their mountain-like San Philip that, of fifteen hundred
    tons,
And up-shadowing high above us with her yawning tiers of
    guns,
Took the breath from our sails, and we stay'd.

And while now the great San Philip hung above us like a
    cloud
Whence the thunderbolt will fall
Long and loud

Four galleons drew away
From the Spanish fleet that day,
And two upon the larboard and two upon the starboard lay,
And the battle-thunder broke from them all.

But anon the great San Philip, she bethought herself and went,
Having that within her womb that had left her ill content;
And the rest they came aboard us, and they fought us hand
    to hand,
For a dozen times they came with their pikes and musque-
    teers,
And a dozen times we shook 'em off as a dog that shakes his
    ears
When he leaps from the water to the land.

And the sun went down, and the stars came out far over the
    summer sea,
But never a moment ceased the fight of the one and the
    fifty-three.
Ship after ship, the whole night long, their high-built galleons
    came,
Ship after ship, the whole night long, with her battle-thunder
    and flame;
Ship after ship, the whole night long, drew back with her dead
    and her shame.
For some were sunk and many were shatter'd, and so could
    fight us no more—
God of battles, was ever a battle like this in the world before?

For he said, 'Fight on! fight on!'
Tho' his vessel was all but a wreck;
And it chanced that, when half of the short summer night was
    gone,
With a grisly wound to be drest he had left the deck,

But a bullet struck him that was dressing it suddenly dead,
And himself he was wounded again in the side and the head,
And he said, 'Fight on! fight on!'

And the night went down, and the sun smiled out far over the
 summer sea,
And the Spanish fleet with broken sides lay round us all in a
 ring;
But they dared not touch us again, for they fear'd that we
 still could sting,
So they watch'd what the end would be.
And we had not fought them in vain,
But in perilous plight were we,
Seeing forty of our poor hundred were slain,
And half of the rest of us maim'd for life
In the crash of the cannonades and the desperate strife;
And the sick men down in the hold were most of them stark
 and cold,
And the pikes were all broken or bent, and the powder was
 all of it spent;
And the masts and the rigging were lying over the side;
But Sir Richard cried in his English pride:
'We have fought such a fight for a day and a night
As may never be fought again!
We have won great glory, my men!
And a day less or more
At sea or ashore,
We die—does it matter when?
Sink me the ship, Master Gunner—sink her, split her in twain!
Fall into the hands of God, not into the hands of Spain!'

And the gunner said, 'Ay, ay,' but the seamen made reply:
'We have children, we have wives,
And the Lord hath spared our lives.

We will make the Spaniard promise, if we yield, to let us go;
We shall live to fight again and to strike another blow.'
And the lion there lay dying, and they yielded to the foe.

And the stately Spanish men to their flagship bore him then,
Where they laid him by the mast, old Sir Richard caught at
    last,
And they praised him to his face with their courtly foreign
    grace;
But he rose upon their decks, and he cried:
'I have fought for Queen and Faith like a valiant man and
    true;
I have only done my duty as a man is bound to do.
With a joyful spirit I Sir Richard Grenville die!'
And he fell upon their decks, and he died.

And they stared at the dead that had been so valiant and true,
And had holden the power and glory of Spain so cheap
That he dared her with one little ship and his English few;
Was he devil or man? He was devil for aught they knew,
But they sank his body with honor down into the deep,
And they mann'd the Revenge with a swarthier alien crew,
And away she sail'd with her loss and long'd for her own;
When a wind from the lands they had ruin'd awoke from
    sleep,
And the water began to heave and the weather to moan,
And or ever that evening ended a great gale blew,
And a wave like the wave that is raised by an earthquake
    grew,
Till it smote on their hulls and their sails and their masts and
    their flags,
And the whole sea plunged and fell on the shot-shatter'd navy
    of Spain,
And the little Revenge herself went down by the island crags
To be lost evermore in the main.

THE CAPTAIN

THE CAPTAIN

A LEGEND OF THE NAVY

HE THAT only rules by terror
　Doeth grievous wrong.
Deep as hell I count his error.
　Let him hear my song.
Brave the Captain was; the seamen
　Made a gallant crew,
Gallant sons of English freemen,
　Sailors bold and true.
But they hated his oppression;
　Stern he was and rash,
So for every light transgression
　Doom'd them to the lash.
Day by day more harsh and cruel
　Seem'd the Captain's mood.
Secret wrath like smother'd fuel
　Burnt in each man's blood.
Yet he hoped to purchase glory,
　Hoped to make the name
Of his vessel great in story,
　Wheresoe'er he came.
So they past by capes and islands,
　Many a harbor-mouth,
Sailing under palmy highlands
　Far within the South.
On a day when they were going
　O'er the lone expanse,
In the north, her canvas flowing,
　Rose a ship of France.
Then the Captain's color heighten'd,
　Joyful came his speech;

But a cloudy gladness lighten'd
  In the eyes of each.
'Chase,' he said; the ship flew forward,
  And the wind did blow;
Stately, lightly, went she norward,
  Till she near'd the foe.
Then they look'd at him they hated,
  Had what they desired;
Mute with folded arms they waited—
  Not a gun was fired.
But they heard the foeman's thunder
  Roaring out their doom;
All the air was torn in sunder,
  Crashing went the boom,
Spars were splinter'd, decks were shatter'd,
  Bullets fell like rain;
Over mast and deck were scatter'd
  Blood and brains of men.
Spars were splinter'd; decks were broken;
  Every mother's son—
Down they dropt—no word was spoken—
  Each beside his gun.
On the decks as they were lying,
  Were their faces grim.
In their blood, as they lay dying,
  Did they smile on him.
Those in whom he had reliance
  For his noble name
With one smile of still defiance
  Sold him unto shame.
Shame and wrath his heart confounded,
  Pale he turn'd and red,
Till himself was deadly wounded
  Falling on the dead.

Dismal error! fearful slaughter!
  Years have wander'd by;
Side by side beneath the water
  Crew and Captain lie;
There the sunlit ocean tosses
  O'er them mouldering,
And the lonely seabird crosses
  With one waft of the wing.

ODE ON THE DEATH OF THE DUKE OF WELLINGTON

Bury the Great Duke
  With an empire's lamentation;
Let us bury the Great Duke
  To the noise of the mourning of a mighty nation;
Mourning when their leaders fall,
Warriors carry the warrior's pall,
And sorrow darkens hamlet and hall.

Where shall we lay the man whom we deplore?
Here, in streaming London's central roar.
Let the sound of those he wrought for,
And the feet of those he fought for,
Echo round his bones for evermore.

Lead out the pageant: sad and slow,
As fits an universal woe,
Let the long, long procession go,
And let the sorrowing crowd about it grow,
And let the mournful martial music blow;
The last great Englishman is low.

Mourn, for to us he seems the last,
Remembering all his greatness in the past.
No more in soldier fashion will he greet
With lifted hand the gazer in the street.
O friends, our chief state-oracle is mute!
Mourn for the man of long-enduring blood,
The statesman-warrior, moderate, resolute,
Whole in himself, a common good.
Mourn for the man of amplest influence,
Yet clearest of ambitious crime,
Our greatest yet with least pretence,
Great in council and great in war,
Foremost captain of his time,
Rich in saving common-sense,
And, as the greatest only are,
In his simplicity sublime.
O good gray head which all men knew,
O voice from which their omens all men drew,
O iron nerve to true occasion true,
O fallen at length that tower of strength
Which stood four-square to all the winds that blew!
Such was he whom we deplore.
The long self-sacrifice of life is o'er.
The great World-victor's victor will be seen no more.

All is over and done.
Render thanks to the Giver,
England, for thy son.
Let the bell be toll'd.
Render thanks to the Giver,
And render him to the mould.
Under the cross of gold
That shines over city and river,
There he shall rest for ever

Among the wise and the bold.
Let the bell be toll'd,
And a reverent people behold
The towering car, the sable steeds.
Bright let it be with its blazon'd deeds,
Dark in its funeral fold.
Let the bell be toll'd,
And a deeper knell in the heart be knoll'd;
And the sound of the sorrowing anthem roll'd
Thro' the dome of the golden cross;
And the volleying cannon thunder his loss;
He knew their voices of old.
For many a time in many a clime
His captain's-ear has heard them boom,
Bellowing victory, bellowing doom.
When he with those deep voices wrought,
Guarding realms and kings from shame,
With those deep voices our dead captain taught
The tyrant, and asserts his claim
In that dread sound to the great name
Which he has worn so pure of blame,
In praise and in dispraise the same,
A man of well-attemper'd frame.
O civic muse, to such a name,
To such a name for ages long,
To such a name,
Preserve a broad approach of fame,
And ever-echoing avenues of song!

'Who is he that cometh, like an honor'd guest,
With banner and with music, with soldier and with priest,
With a nation weeping, and breaking on my rest?'—
Mighty Seaman, this is he
Was great by land as thou by sea.

Thine island loves thee well, thou famous man,
The greatest sailor since our world began.
Now, to the roll of muffled drums,
To thee the greatest soldier comes;
For this is he
Was great by land as thou by sea.
His foes were thine; he kept us free;
O, give him welcome, this is he
Worthy of our gorgeous rites,
And worthy to be laid by thee;
For this is England's greatest son,
He that gain'd a hundred fights,
Nor ever lost an English gun;
This is he that far away
Against the myriads of Assaye
Clash'd with his fiery few and won;
And underneath another sun,
Warring on a later day,
Round affrighted Lisbon drew
The treble works, the vast designs
Of his labor'd rampart-lines,
Where he greatly stood at bay,
Whence he issued forth anew,
And ever great and greater grew,
Beating from the wasted vines
Back to France her banded swarms,
Back to France with countless blows,
Till o'er the hills her eagles flew
Beyond the Pyrenean pines,
Follow'd up in valley and glen
With blare of bugle, clamor of men,
Roll of cannon and clash of arms,
And England pouring on her foes.

Such a war had such a close.
Again their ravening eagle rose
In anger, wheel'd on Europe-shadowing wings,
And barking for the thrones of kings;
Till one that sought but Duty's iron crown
On that loud Sabbath shook the spoiler down;
A day of onsets of despair!
Dash'd on every rocky square,
Their surging charges foam'd themselves away;
Last, the Prussian trumpet blew;
Thro' the long-tormented air
Heaven flash'd a sudden jubilant ray,
And down we swept and charged and overthrew.
So great a soldier taught us there
What long-enduring hearts could do
In that world-earthquake, Waterloo!
Mighty Seaman, tender and true,
And pure as he from taint of craven guile,
O saviour of the silver-coasted isle,
O shaker of the Baltic and the Nile,
If aught of things that here befall
Touch a spirit among things divine,
If love of country move thee there at all,
Be glad, because his bones are laid by thine!
And thro' the centuries let a people's voice
In full acclaim,
A people's voice,
The proof and echo of all human fame,
A people's voice, when they rejoice
At civic revel and pomp and game,
Attest their great commander's claim
With honor, honor, honor, honor to him,
Eternal honor to his name.

A people's voice! we are a people yet.
Tho' all men else their nobler dreams forget,
Confused by brainless mobs and lawless Powers,
Thank Him who isled us here, and roughly set
His Briton in blown seas and storming showers,
We have a voice with which to pay the debt
Of boundless love and reverence and regret
To those great men who fought, and kept it ours.
And keep it ours, O God, from brute control!
O Statesmen, guard us, guard the eye, the soul
Of Europe, keep our noble England whole,
And save the one true seed of freedom sown
Betwixt a people and their ancient throne,
That sober freedom out of which there springs
Our loyal passion for our temperate kings!
For, saving that, ye help to save mankind
Till public wrong be crumbled into dust,
And drill the raw world for the march of mind,
Till crowds at length be sane and crowns be just.
But wink no more in slothful over-trust.
Remember him who led your hosts;
He bade you guard the sacred coasts.
Your cannons moulder on the seaward wall;
His voice is silent in your council-hall
For ever; and whatever tempests lour
For ever silent; even if they broke
In thunder, silent; yet remember all
He spoke among you, and the Man who spoke;
Who never sold the truth to serve the hour,
Nor palter'd with Eternal God for power;
Who let the turbid streams of rumor flow
Thro' either babbling world of high and low;
Whose life was work, whose language rife
With rugged maxims hewn from life;

Who never spoke against a foe;
Whose eighty winters freeze with one rebuke
All great self-seekers trampling on the right.
Truth-teller was our England's Alfred named;
Truth-lover was our English Duke;
Whatever record leap to light
He never shall be shamed.

Lo! the leader in these glorious wars
Now to glorious burial slowly borne,
Follow'd by the brave of other lands,
He, on whom from both her open hands
Lavish Honor shower'd all her stars,
And affluent Fortune emptied all her horn.
Yea, let all good things await
Him who cares not to be great
But as he saves or serves the state.
Not once or twice in our rough island-story
The path of duty was the way to glory.
He that walks it, only thirsting
For the right, and learns to deaden
Love of self, before his journey closes,
He shall find the stubborn thistle bursting
Into glossy purples, which outredden
All voluptuous garden-roses.
Not once or twice in our fair island story
The path of duty was the way to glory.
He, that ever following her commands,
On with toil of heart and knees and hands,
Thro' the long gorge to the far light has won
His path upward, and prevail'd,
Shall find the toppling crags of Duty scaled
Are close upon the shining table-lands

To which our God Himself is moon and sun.
Such was he: his work is done.
But while the races of mankind endure
Let his great example stand
Colossal, seen of every land,
And keep the soldier firm, the statesman pure;
Till in all lands and thro' all human story
The path of duty be the way to glory.
And let the land whose hearths he saved from shame
For many and many an age proclaim
At civic revel and pomp and game,
And when the long-illumined cities flame,
Their ever-loyal iron leader's fame,
With honor, honor, honor, honor to him,
Eternal honor to his name.

Peace, his triumph will be sung
By some yet unmoulded tongue
Far on in summers that we shall not see.
Peace, it is a day of pain
For one about whose patriarchal knee
Late the little children clung.
O peace, it is a day of pain
For one upon whose hand and heart and brain
Once the weight and fate of Europe hung.
Ours the pain, be his the gain!
More than is of man's degree
Must be with us, watching here
At this, our great solemnity.
Whom we see not we revere;
We revere, and we refrain
From talk of battles loud and vain,
And brawling memories all too free

For such a wise humility
As befits a solemn fane:
We revere, and while we hear
The tides of Music's golden sea
Setting toward eternity,
Uplifted high in heart and hope are we,
Until we doubt not that for one so true
There must be other nobler work to do
Than when he fought at Waterloo,
And Victor he must ever be.
For tho' the Giant Ages heave the hill
And break the shore, and evermore
Make and break, and work their will,
Tho' world on world in myriad myriads roll
Round us each with different powers,
And other forms of life than ours,
What know we greater than the soul?
On God and Godlike men we build our trust.
Hush, the Dead March wails in the people's ears;
The dark crowd moves, and there are sobs and tears;
The black earth yawns; the mortal disappears;
Ashes to ashes, dust to dust;
He is gone who seem'd so great.—
Gone, but nothing can bereave him
Of the force he made his own
Being here, and we believe him
Something far advanced in State,
And that he wears a truer crown
Than any wreath that man can weave him.
Speak no more of his renown,
Lay your earthly fancies down,
And in the vast cathedral leave him,
God accept him, Christ receive him!

THE CHARGE OF THE LIGHT BRIGADE

HALF a league, half a league,
Half a league onward,
All in the valley of Death
  Rode the six hundred.
'Forward the Light Brigade!
Charge for the guns!' he said.
Into the valley of Death
  Rode the six hundred.

'Forward, the Light Brigade!'
Was there a man dismay'd?
Not tho' the soldier knew
  Some one had blunder'd.
Theirs not to make reply,
Theirs not to reason why,
Theirs but to do and die.
Into the valley of Death
  Rode the six hundred.

Cannon to right of them,
Cannon to left of them,
Cannon in front of them
  Volley'd and thunder'd;
Storm'd at with shot and shell,
Boldly they rode and well,
Into the jaws of Death,
Into the mouth of hell
  Rode the six hundred.

Flash'd all their sabres bare,
Flash'd as they turn'd in air
Sabring the gunners there,
Charging an army, while
  All the world wonder'd.

Plunged in the battery smoke
Right thro' the line they broke.
Cossack and Russian
Reel'd from the sabre-stroke
  Shatter'd and sunder'd.
Then they rode back, but not,
  Not the six hundred.

Cannon to right of them,
Cannon to left of them,
Cannon behind them
  Volley'd and thunder'd;
Storm'd at with shot and shell,
While horse and hero fell,
They that had fought so well
Came thro' the jaws of Death,
Back from the mouth of hell,
All that was left of them,
  Left of six hundred.

When can their glory fade?
O the wild charge they made!
  All the world wonder'd.
Honor the charge they made!
Honor the Light Brigade,
  Noble six hundred!

'YOU ASK ME, WHY, THO' ILL AT EASE'

You ask me, why, tho' ill at ease,
  Within this region I subsist,
  Whose spirits falter in the mist,
And languish for the purple seas.

It is the land that freemen till,
  That sober-suited Freedom chose,
  The land, where girt with friends or foes
A man may speak the thing he will;

A land of settled government,
  A land of just and old renown,
  Where Freedom slowly broadens down
From precedent to precedent;

Where faction seldom gathers head,
  But, by degrees to fullness wrought,
  The strength of some diffusive thought
Hath time and space to work and spread.

Should banded unions persecute
  Opinion, and induce a time
  When single thought is civil crime,
And individual freedom mute,

Tho' power should make from land to land
  The name of Britain trebly great—
  Tho' every channel of the State
Should fill and choke with golden sand—

Yet waft me from the harbor-mouth,
  Wild wind! I seek a warmer sky,
  And I will see before I die
The palms and temples of the South.

'OF OLD SAT FREEDOM ON THE HEIGHTS'

OF OLD sat Freedom on the heights,
  The thunders breaking at her feet;
Above her shook the starry lights;
  She heard the torrents meet.

There in her place she did rejoice,
  Self-gather'd in her prophet-mind,
But fragments of her mighty voice
  Came rolling on the wind.

Then stept she down thro' town and field
  To mingle with the human race,
And part by part to men reveal'd
  The fullness of her face—

Grave mother of majestic works,
  From her isle-altar gazing down,
Who, Godlike, grasps the triple forks,
  And, king-like, wears the crown.

Her open eyes desire the truth.
  The wisdom of a thousand years
Is in them. May perpetual youth
  Keep dry their light from tears;

That her fair form may stand and shine,
  Make bright our days and light our dreams,
Turning to scorn with lips divine
  The falsehood of extremes!

IDYLLS

ENOCH ARDEN

LONG lines of cliff breaking have left a chasm;
And in the chasm are foam and yellow sands;
Beyond, red roofs about a narrow wharf
In cluster; then a moulder'd church; and higher
A long street climbs to one tall-tower'd mill;
And high in heaven behind it a gray down
With Danish barrows; and a hazelwood,
By autumn nutters haunted, flourishes
Green in a cuplike hollow of the down.
Here on this beach a hundred years ago,
Three children of three houses, Annie Lee,
The prettiest little damsel in the port,
And Philip Ray, the miller's only son,
And Enoch Arden, a rough sailor's lad
Made orphan by a winter shipwreck, play'd
Among the waste and lumber of the shore,
Hard coils of cordage, swarthy fishing-nets,
Anchors of rusty fluke, and boats updrawn;
And built their castles of dissolving sand
To watch them overflow'd, or following up
And flying the white breaker, daily left
The little footprint daily wash'd away.

A narrow cave ran in beneath the cliff;
In this the children play'd at keeping house.
Enoch was host one day, Philip the next,

While Annie still was mistress; but at times
Enoch would hold possession for a week:
'This is my house and this my little wife,'
'Mine too,' said Philip; 'turn and turn about;'
When, if they quarrell'd, Enoch stronger-made
Was master. Then would Philip, his blue eyes
All flooded with the helpless wrath of tears,
Shriek out, 'I hate you, Enoch,' and at this
The little wife would weep for company,
And pray them not to quarrel for her sake,
And say she would be little wife to both.

But when the dawn of rosy childhood past,
And the new warmth of life's ascending sun
Was felt by either, either fixt his heart
On that one girl; and Enoch spoke his love,
But Philip loved in silence; and the girl
Seem'd kinder unto Philip than to him;
But she loved Enoch, tho' she knew it not,
And would if ask'd deny it. Enoch set
A purpose evermore before his eyes,
To hoard all savings to the uttermost,
To purchase his own boat, and make a home
For Annie; and so prosper'd that at last
A luckier or a bolder fisherman,
A carefuller in peril, did not breathe
For leagues along that breaker-beaten coast
Than Enoch. Likewise had he served a year
On board a merchantman, and made himself
Full sailor; and he thrice had pluck'd a life
From the dread sweep of the down-streaming seas,
And all men look'd upon him favorably.
And ere he touch'd his one-and-twentieth May
He purchased his own boat, and made a home

For Annie, neat and nestlike, halfway up
The narrow street that clamber'd toward the mill.

Then, on a golden autumn eventide,
The younger people making holiday,
With bag and sack and basket, great and small,
Went nutting to the hazels. Philip stay'd—
His father lying sick and needing him—
An hour behind; but as he climb'd the hill,
Just where the prone edge of the wood began
To feather toward the hollow, saw the pair,
Enoch and Annie, sitting hand-in-hand,
His large gray eyes and weather-beaten face
All-kindled by a still and sacred fire,
That burn'd as on an altar. Philip look'd,
And in their eyes and faces read his doom;
Then, as their faces drew together, groan'd,
And slipt aside, and like a wounded life
Crept down into the hollows of the wood;
There, while the rest were loud in merry-making,
Had his dark hour unseen, and rose and past
Bearing a lifelong hunger in his heart.

So these were wed, and merrily rang the bells,
And merrily ran the years, seven happy years,
Seven happy years of health and competence,
And mutual love and honorable toil,
With children, first a daughter. In him woke,
With his first babe's first cry, the noble wish
To save all earnings to the uttermost,
And give his child a better bringing-up
Than his had been, or hers; a wish renew'd,
When two years after came a boy to be
The rosy idol of her solitudes,

While Enoch was abroad on wrathful seas,
Or often journeying landward; for in truth
Enoch's white horse, and Enoch's ocean-spoil
In ocean-smelling osier, and his face,
Rough-redden'd with a thousand winter gales,
Not only to the market-cross were known,
But in the leafy lanes behind the down,
Far as the portal-warding lion-whelp
And Peacock yew-tree of the lonely Hall,
Whose Friday fare was Enoch's ministering.

Then came a change, as all things human change.
Ten miles to northward of the narrow port
Open'd a larger haven. Thither used
Enoch at times to go by land or sea;
And once when there, and clambering on a mast
In harbor, by mischance he slipt and fell.
A limb was broken when they lifted him;
And while he lay recovering there, his wife
Bore him another son, a sickly one.
Another hand crept too across his trade
Taking her bread and theirs; and on him fell,
Altho' a grave and staid God-fearing man,
Yet lying thus inactive, doubt and gloom.
He seem'd, as in a nightmare of the night,
To see his children leading evermore
Low miserable lives of hand-to-mouth,
And her he loved a beggar. Then he pray'd,
'Save them from this, whatever comes to me.'
And while he pray'd, the master of that ship
Enoch had served in, hearing his mischance,
Came, for he knew the man and valued him,
Reporting of his vessel China-bound,
And wanting yet a boatswain. Would he go?

There yet were many weeks before she sail'd,
Sail'd from this port. Would Enoch have the place?
And Enoch all at once assented to it,
Rejoicing at that answer to his prayer.

So now that shadow of mischance appear'd
No graver than as when some little cloud
Cuts off the fiery highway of the sun,
And isles a light in the offing. Yet the wife—
When he was gone—the children—what to do?
Then Enoch lay long-pondering on his plans:
To sell the boat—and yet he loved her well—
How many a rough sea had he weather'd in her!
He knew her, as a horseman knows his horse—
And yet to sell her—then with what she brought
Buy goods and stores—set Annie forth in trade
With all that seamen needed or their wives—
So might she keep the house while he was gone.
Should he not trade himself out yonder? go
This voyage more than once? yea, twice or thrice—
As oft as needed—last, returning rich,
Become the master of a larger craft,
With fuller profits lead an easier life,
Have all his pretty young ones educated,
And pass his days in peace among his own.

Thus Enoch in his heart determined all;
Then moving homeward came on Annie pale,
Nursing the sickly babe, her latest-born.
Forward she started with a happy cry,
And laid the feeble infant in his arms;
Whom Enoch took, and handled all his limbs,
Appraised his weight and fondled fatherlike,
But had no heart to break his purposes
To Annie, till the morrow, when he spoke.

Then first since Enoch's golden ring had girt
Her finger, Annie fought against his will;
Yet not with brawling opposition she,
But manifold entreaties, many a tear,
Many a sad kiss by day, by night, renew'd—
Sure that all evil would come out of it—
Besought him, supplicating, if he cared
For her or his dear children, not to go.
He not for his own self caring, but her,
Her and her children, let her plead in vain;
So grieving held his will, and bore it thro'.

For Enoch parted with his old sea-friend,
Bought Annie goods and stores, and set his hand
To fit their little streetward sitting-room
With shelf and corner for the goods and stores.
So all day long till Enoch's last at home,
Shaking their pretty cabin, hammer and axe,
Auger and saw, while Annie seem'd to hear
Her own death-scaffold raising, shrill'd and rang,
Till this was ended, and his careful hand,—
The space was narrow,—having order'd all
Almost as neat and close as Nature packs
Her blossom or her seedling, paused, and he,
Who needs would work for Annie to the last,
Ascending tired, heavily slept till morn.

And Enoch faced this morning of farewell
Brightly and boldly. All his Annie's fears,
Save as his Annie's, were a laughter to him.
Yet Enoch as a brave God-fearing man
Bow'd himself down, and in that mystery
Where God-in-man is one with man-in-God,
Pray'd for a blessing on his wife and babes,

Whatever came to him; and then he said:
'Annie, this voyage by the grace of God
Will bring fair weather yet to all of us.
Keep a clean hearth and a clear fire for me,
For I 'll be back, my girl, before you know it;'
Then lightly rocking baby's cradle, 'and he,
This pretty, puny, weakly little one,—
Nay—for I love him all the better for it—
God bless him, he shall sit upon my knees
And I will tell him tales of foreign parts,
And make him merry, when I come home again.
Come, Annie, come, cheer up before I go.'

   Him running on thus hopefully she heard,
And almost hoped herself; but when he turn'd
The current of his talk to graver things
In sailor fashion roughly sermonizing
On providence and trust in heaven, she heard,
Heard and not heard him; as the village girl,
Who sets her pitcher underneath the spring,
Musing on him that used to fill it for her,
Hears and not hears, and lets it overflow.

   At length she spoke: 'O Enoch, you are wise;
And yet for all your wisdom well know I
That I shall look upon your face no more.'

   'Well, then,' said Enoch, 'I shall look on yours.
Annie, the ship I sail in passes here'—
He named the day;—'get you a seaman's glass,
Spy out my face, and laugh at all your fears.'

   But when the last of those last moments came:
'Annie, my girl, cheer up, be comforted,
Look to the babes, and till I come again

Keep everything shipshape, for I must go.
And fear no more for me; or if you fear,
Cast all your cares on God; that anchor holds.
Is He not yonder in those uttermost
Parts of the morning? if I flee to these,
Can I go from Him? and the sea is His,
The sea is His; He made it.'

        Enoch rose,
Cast his strong arms about his drooping wife,
And kiss'd his wonder-stricken little ones;
But for the third, the sickly one, who slept
After a night of feverous wakefulness,
When Annie would have raised him Enoch said,
'Wake him not, let him sleep; how should the child
Remember this?' and kiss'd him in his cot.
But Annie from her baby's forehead clipt
A tiny curl, and gave it; this he kept
Thro' all his future, but now hastily caught
His bundle, waved his hand, and went his way.

 She, when the day that Enoch mention'd came,
Borrow'd a glass, but all in vain. Perhaps
She could not fix the glass to suit her eye;
Perhaps her eye was dim, hand tremulous;
She saw him not, and while he stood on deck
Waving, the moment and the vessel past.

 Even to the last dip of the vanishing sail
She watch'd it, and departed weeping for him;
Then, tho' she mourn'd his absence as his grave,
Set her sad will no less to chime with his,
But throve not in her trade, not being bred
To barter, nor compensating the want

By shrewdness, neither capable of lies,
Nor asking overmuch and taking less,
And still foreboding 'what would Enoch say?'
For more than once, in days of difficulty
And pressure, had she sold her wares for less
Than what she gave in buying what she sold.
She fail'd and sadden'd knowing it; and thus,
Expectant of that news which never came,
Gain'd for her own a scanty sustenance,
And lived a life of silent melancholy.

Now the third child was sickly-born and grew
Yet sicklier, tho' the mother cared for it
With all a mother's care; nevertheless,
Whether her business often call'd her from it,
Or thro' the want of what it needed most,
Or means to pay the voice who best could tell
What most it needed—howsoe'er it was,
After a lingering,—ere she was aware,—
Like the caged bird escaping suddenly,
The little innocent soul flitted away.

In that same week when Annie buried it,
Philip's true heart, which hunger'd for her peace,—
Since Enoch left he had not look'd upon her,—
Smote him, as having kept aloof so long.
'Surely,' said Philip, 'I may see her now,
May be some little comfort;' therefore went,
Past thro' the solitary room in front,
Paused for a moment at an inner door,
Then struck it thrice, and, no one opening,
Enter'd, but Annie, seated with her grief,
Fresh from the burial of her little one,

Cared not to look on any human face,
But turn'd her own toward the wall and wept.
Then Philip standing up said falteringly,
'Annie, I came to ask a favor of you.'

He spoke; the passion in her moan'd reply,
'Favor from one so sad and so forlorn
As I am!' half abash'd him; yet unask'd,
His bashfulness and tenderness at war,
He set himself beside her, saying to her:

'I came to speak to you of what he wish'd,
Enoch, your husband. I have ever said
You chose the best among us—a strong man;
For where he fixt his heart he set his hand
To do the thing he will'd, and bore it thro'.
And wherefore did he go this weary way,
And leave you lonely? not to see the world—
For pleasure?—nay, but for the wherewithal
To give his babes a better bringing up
Than his had been, or yours; that was his wish.
And if he come again, vext will he be
To find the precious morning hours were lost.
And it would vex him even in his grave,
If he could know his babes were running wild
Like colts about the waste. So, Annie, now—
Have we not known each other all our lives?
I do beseech you by the love you bear
Him and his children not to say me nay—
For, if you will, when Enoch comes again
Why then he shall repay me—if you will,
Annie—for I am rich and well-to-do.
Now let me put the boy and girl to school;
This is the favor that I came to ask.'

Then Annie with her brows against the wall
Answer'd, 'I cannot look you in the face;
I seem so foolish and so broken down.
When you came in my sorrow broke me down;
And now I think your kindness breaks me down.
But Enoch lives; that is borne in on me;
He will repay you. Money can be repaid,
Not kindness such as yours.'

    And Philip ask'd,
'Then you will let me, Annie?'

    There she turn'd,
She rose, and fixt her swimming eyes upon him,
And dwelt a moment on his kindly face,
Then calling down a blessing on his head
Caught at his hand, and wrung it passionately,
And past into the little garth beyond.
So lifted up in spirit he moved away.

Then Philip put the boy and girl to school,
And bought them needful books, and every way,
Like one who does his duty by his own,
Made himself theirs; and tho' for Annie's sake,
Fearing the lazy gossip of the port,
He oft denied his heart his dearest wish,
And seldom crost her threshold, yet he sent
Gifts by the children, garden-herbs and fruit,
The late and early roses from his wall,
Or conies from the down, and now and then,
With some pretext of fineness in the meal
To save the offence of charitable, flour
From his tall mill that whistled on the waste.

But Philip did not fathom Annie's mind;
Scarce could the woman, when he came upon her,
Out of full heart and boundless gratitude
Light on a broken word to thank him with.
But Philip was her children's all-in-all;
From distant corners of the street they ran
To greet his hearty welcome heartily;
Lords of his house and of his mill were they,
Worried his passive ear with petty wrongs
Or pleasures, hung upon him, play'd with him
And call'd him Father Philip. Philip gain'd
As Enoch lost, for Enoch seem'd to them
Uncertain as a vision or a dream,
Faint as a figure seen in early dawn
Down at the far end of an avenue,
Going we know not where; and so ten years,
Since Enoch left his hearth and native land,
Fled forward, and no news of Enoch came.

It chanced one evening Annie's children long'd
To go with others nutting to the wood,
And Annie would go with them; then they begg'd
For Father Philip, as they call'd him, too.
Him, like the working bee in blossom dust,
Blanch'd with his mill, they found; and saying to him,
'Come with us, Father Philip,' he denied;
But when the children pluck'd at him to go,
He laugh'd, and yielded readily to their wish,
For was not Annie with them? and they went.

But after scaling half the weary down,
Just where the prone edge of the wood began
To feather toward the hollow, all her force
Fail'd her; and sighing, 'Let me rest,' she said,

So Philip rested with her well-content;
While all the younger ones with jubilant cries
Broke from their elders, and tumultuously
Down thro' the whitening hazels made a plunge
To the bottom, and dispersed, and bent or broke
The lithe reluctant boughs to tear away
Their tawny clusters, crying to each other
And calling, here and there, about the wood.

But Philip sitting at her side forgot
Her presence, and remember'd one dark hour
Here in this wood, when like a wounded life
He crept into the shadow. At last he said,
Lifting his honest forehead, 'Listen, Annie,
How merry they are down yonder in the wood.
Tired, Annie?' for she did not speak a word.
'Tired?' but her face had fallen upon her hands;
At which, as with a kind of anger in him,
'The ship was lost,' he said, 'the ship was lost!
No more of that! why should you kill yourself
And make them orphans quite?' And Annie said,
'I thought not of it; but—I know not why—
Their voices make me feel so solitary.'

Then Philip coming somewhat closer spoke:
'Annie, there is a thing upon my mind,
And it has been upon my mind so long
That, tho' I know not when it first came there,
I know that it will out at last. O Annie,
It is beyond all hope, against all chance,
That he who left you ten long years ago
Should still be living; well, then—let me speak.
I grieve to see you poor and wanting help;
I cannot help you as I wish to do

Unless—they say that women are so quick—
Perhaps you know what I would have you know—
I wish you for my wife. I fain would prove
A father to your children; I do think
They love me as a father; I am sure
That I love them as if they were mine own;
And I believe, if you were fast my wife,
That after all these sad uncertain years
We might be still as happy as God grants
To any of his creatures. Think upon it;
For I am well-to-do—no kin, no care,
No burthen, save my care for you and yours,
And we have known each other all our lives,
And I have loved you longer than you know.'

   Then answer'd Annie—tenderly she spoke:
'You have been as God's good angel in our house.
God bless you for it, God reward you for it,
Philip, with something happier than myself.
Can one love twice? can you be ever loved
As Enoch was? what is it that you ask?'
'I am content,' he answer'd, 'to be loved
A little after Enoch.' 'O,' she cried,
Scared as it were, 'dear Philip, wait a while.
If Enoch comes—but Enoch will not come—
Yet wait a year, a year is not so long.
Surely I shall be wiser in a year.
O, wait a little!' Philip sadly said,
'Annie, as I have waited all my life
I well may wait a little.' 'Nay,' she cried,
'I am bound: you have my promise—in a year.
Will you not bide your year as I bide mine?'
And Philip answer'd, 'I will bide my year.'

Here both were mute, till Philip glancing up
Beheld the dead flame of the fallen day
Pass from the Danish barrow overhead;
Then, fearing night and chill for Annie, rose
And sent his voice beneath him thro' the wood.
Up came the children laden with their spoil;
Then all descended to the port, and there
At Annie's door he paused and gave his hand,
Saying gently, 'Annie, when I spoke to you,
That was your hour of weakness. I was wrong,
I am always bound to you, but you are free.'
Then Annie weeping answer'd, 'I am bound.'

She spoke; and in one moment as it were,
While yet she went about her household ways,
Even as she dwelt upon his latest words,
That he had loved her longer than she knew,
That autumn into autumn flash'd again,
And there he stood once more before her face,
Claiming her promise. 'Is it a year?' she ask'd.
'Yes, if the nuts,' he said, 'be ripe again;
Come out and see.' But she—she put him off—
So much to look to—such a change—a month—
Give her a month—she knew that she was bound—
A month—no more. Then Philip with his eyes
Full of that lifelong hunger, and his voice
Shaking a little like a drunkard's hand,
'Take your own time, Annie, take your own time.'
And Annie could have wept for pity of him;
And yet she held him on delayingly
With many a scarce-believable excuse,
Trying his truth and his long-sufferance,
Till half another year had slipt away.

By this the lazy gossips of the port,
Abhorrent of a calculation crost,
Began to chafe as at a personal wrong.
Some thought that Philip did but trifle with her;
Some that she but held off to draw him on;
And others laugh'd at her and Philip too,
As simple folk that knew not their own minds;
And one, in whom all evil fancies clung
Like serpent eggs together, laughingly
Would hint at worse in either. Her own son
Was silent, tho' he often look'd his wish;
But evermore the daughter prest upon her
To wed the man so dear to all of them
And lift the household out of poverty;
And Philip's rosy face contracting grew
Careworn and wan; and all these things fell on her
Sharp as reproach.

    At last one night it chanced
That Annie could not sleep, but earnestly
Pray'd for a sign, 'My Enoch, is he gone?'
Then compass'd round by the blind wall of night
Brook'd not the expectant terror of her heart,
Started from bed, and struck herself a light,
Then desperately seized the holy Book,
Suddenly set it wide to find a sign,
Suddenly put her finger on the text,
'Under the palm-tree.' That was nothing to her,
No meaning there; she closed the Book and slept.
When lo! her Enoch sitting on a height,
Under a palm-tree, over him the sun.
'He is gone,' she thought, 'he is happy, he is singing
Hosanna in the highest; yonder shines
The Sun of Righteousness, and these be palms

Whereof the happy people strowing cried
"Hosanna in the highest!" ' Here she woke,
Resolved, sent for him and said wildly to him,
'There is no reason why we should not wed.'
'Then for God's sake,' he answer'd, 'both our sakes,
So you will wed me, let it be at once.'

 So these were wed, and merrily rang the bells,
Merrily rang the bells, and they were wed.
But never merrily beat Annie's heart.
A footstep seem'd to fall beside her path,
She knew not whence; a whisper on her ear,
She knew not what; nor loved she to be left
Alone at home, nor ventured out alone.
What ail'd her then that, ere she enter'd, often
Her hand dwelt lingeringly on the latch,
Fearing to enter? Philip thought he knew:
Such doubts and fears were common to her state,
Being with child; but when her child was born,
Then her new child was as herself renew'd,
Then the new mother came about her heart,
Then her good Philip was her all-in-all,
And that mysterious instinct wholly died.

 And where was Enoch? Prosperously sail'd
The ship 'Good Fortune,' tho' at setting forth
The Biscay, roughly ridging eastward, shook
And almost overwhelm'd her, yet unvext
She slipt across the summer of the world,
Then after a long tumble about the Cape
And frequent interchange of foul and fair,
She passing thro' the summer world again,
The breath of heaven came continually
And sent her sweetly by the golden isles,
Till silent in her oriental haven.

There Enoch traded for himself, and bought
Quaint monsters for the market of those times,
A gilded dragon also for the babes.

Less lucky her home-voyage: at first indeed
Thro' many a fair sea-circle, day by day,
Scarce-rocking, her full-busted figurehead
Stared o'er the ripple feathering from her bows:
Then follow'd calms, and then winds variable,
Then baffling, a long course of them; and last
Storm, such as drove her under moonless heavens
Till hard upon the cry of 'breakers' came
The crash of ruin, and the loss of all
But Enoch and two others. Half the night,
Buoy'd upon floating tackle and broken spars,
These drifted, stranding on an isle at morn
Rich, but the loneliest in a lonely sea.

No want was there of human sustenance,
Soft fruitage, mighty nuts, and nourishing roots;
Nor save for pity was it hard to take
The helpless life so wild that it was tame.
There in a seaward-gazing mountain-gorge
They built, and thatch'd with leaves of palm, a hut,
Half hut, half native cavern. So the three,
Set in this Eden of all plenteousness,
Dwelt with eternal summer, ill-content.
For one, the youngest, hardly more than boy,
Hurt in that night of sudden ruin and wreck,
Lay lingering out a five-years' death-in-life.
They could not leave him. After he was gone,
The two remaining found a fallen stem;
And Enoch's comrade, careless of himself,
Fire-hollowing this in Indian fashion, fell

Sun-stricken, and that other lived alone.
In those two deaths he read God's warning 'wait.'

The mountain wooded to the peak, the lawns
And winding glades high up like ways to heaven,
The slender coco's drooping crown of plumes,
The lightning flash of insect and of bird,
The lustre of the long convolvuluses
That coil'd around the stately stems, and ran
Even to the limit of the land, the glows
And glories of the broad belt of the world,—
All these he saw; but what he fain had seen
He could not see, the kindly human face,
Nor ever hear a kindly voice, but heard
The myriad shriek of wheeling ocean-fowl,
The league-long roller thundering on the reef,
The moving whisper of huge trees that branch'd
And blossom'd in the zenith, or the sweep
Of some precipitous rivulet to the wave,
As down the shore he ranged, or all day long
Sat often in the seaward-gazing gorge,
A shipwreck'd sailor, waiting for a sail.
No sail from day to day, but every day
The sunrise broken into scarlet shafts
Among the palms and ferns and precipices;
The blaze upon the waters to the east;
The blaze upon his island overhead;
The blaze upon the waters to the west;
Then the great stars that globed themselves in heaven,
The hollower-bellowing ocean, and again
The scarlet shafts of sunrise—but no sail.

There often as he watch'd or seem'd to watch,
So still the golden lizard on him paused,

A phantom made of many phantoms moved
Before him haunting him, or he himself
Moved haunting people, things, and places, known
Far in a darker isle beyond the line;
The babes, their babble, Annie, the small house,
The climbing street, the mill, the leafy lanes,
The peacock yew-tree and the lonely Hall,
The horse he drove, the boat he sold, the chill
November dawns and dewy-glooming downs,
The gentle shower, the smell of dying leaves,
And the low moan of leaden-color'd seas.

Once likewise, in the ringing of his ears,
Tho' faintly, merrily—far and far away—
He heard the pealing of his parish bells;
Then, tho' he knew not wherefore, started up
Shuddering, and when the beauteous hateful isle
Return'd upon him, had not his poor heart
Spoken with That which being everywhere
Lets none who speaks with Him seem all alone,
Surely the man had died of solitude.

Thus over Enoch's early-silvering head
The sunny and rainy seasons came and went
Year after year. His hopes to see his own,
And pace the sacred old familiar fields,
Not yet had perish'd, when his lonely doom
Came suddenly to an end. Another ship—
She wanted water—blown by baffling winds,
Like the 'Good Fortune,' from her destined course,
Stay'd by this isle, not knowing where she lay;
For since the mate had seen at early dawn
Across a break on the mist-wreathen isle
The silent water slipping from the hills,

They sent a crew that landing burst away
In search of stream or fount, and fill'd the shores
With clamor. Downward from his mountain gorge
Stept the long-hair'd, long-bearded solitary,
Brown, looking hardly human, strangely clad,
Muttering and mumbling, idiot-like it seem'd,
With inarticulate rage, and making signs
They knew not what; and yet he led the way
To where the rivulets of sweet water ran,
And ever as he mingled with the crew,
And heard them talking, his long-bounden tongue
Was loosen'd, till he made them understand;
Whom, when their casks were fill'd, they took aboard.
And there the tale he utter'd brokenly,
Scarce-credited at first but more and more,
Amazed and melted all who listen'd to it;
And clothes they gave him and free passage home,
But oft he work'd among the rest and shook
His isolation from him. None of these
Came from his country, or could answer him,
If question'd, aught of what he cared to know.
And dull the voyage was with long delays,
The vessel scarce sea-worthy; but evermore
His fancy fled before the lazy wind
Returning, till beneath a clouded moon
He like a lover down thro' all his blood
Drew in the dewy meadowy morning-breath
Of England, blown across her ghostly wall.
And that same morning officers and men
Levied a kindly tax upon themselves,
Pitying the lonely man, and gave him it;
Then moving up the coast they landed him,
Even in that harbor whence he sail'd before.

There Enoch spoke no word to any one,
But homeward—home—what home? had he a home?—
His home, he walk'd. Bright was that afternoon,
Sunny but chill; till drawn thro' either chasm,
Where either haven open'd on the deeps,
Roll'd a sea-haze and whelm'd the world in gray,
Cut off the length of highway on before,
And left but narrow breadth to left and right
Of wither'd holt or tilth or pasturage.
On the nigh-naked tree the robin piped
Disconsolate, and thro' the dripping haze
The dead weight of the dead leaf bore it down.
Thicker the drizzle grew, deeper the gloom;
Last, as it seem'd, a great mist-blotted light
Flared on him, and he came upon the place.

Then down the long street having slowly stolen,
His heart foreshadowing all calamity,
His eyes upon the stones, he reach'd the home
Where Annie lived and loved him, and his babes
In those far-off seven happy years were born;
But finding neither light nor murmur there—
A bill of sale gleam'd thro' the drizzle—crept
Still downward thinking, 'dead or dead to me!'

Down to the pool and narrow wharf he went,
Seeking a tavern which of old he knew,
A front of timber-crost antiquity,
So propt, worm-eaten, ruinously old,
He thought it must have gone; but he was gone
Who kept it, and his widow Miriam Lane,
With daily-dwindling profits held the house;
A haunt of brawling seamen once, but now
Stiller, with yet a bed for wandering men.
There Enoch rested silent many days.

But Miriam Lane was good and garrulous,
Nor let him be, but often breaking in,
Told him, with other annals of the port,
Not knowing—Enoch was so brown, so bow'd,
So broken—all the story of his house:
His baby's death, her growing poverty,
How Philip put her little ones to school,
And kept them in it, his long wooing her,
Her slow consent and marriage, and the birth
Of Philip's child; and o'er his countenance
No shadow past, nor mötion. Any one,
Regarding, well had deem'd he felt the tale
Less than the teller; only when she closed,
'Enoch, poor man, was cast away and lost,'
He, shaking his gray head pathetically,
Repeated muttering, 'cast away and lost;'
Again in deeper inward whispers, 'lost!'

But Enoch yearn'd to see her face again:
'If I might look on her sweet face again,
And know that she is happy.' So the thought
Haunted and harass'd him, and drove him forth,
At evening when the dull November day
Was growing duller twilight, to the hill.
There he sat down gazing on all below;
There did a thousand memories roll upon him,
Unspeakable for sadness. By and by
The ruddy square of comfortable light,
Far-blazing from the rear of Philip's house,
Allured him, as the beacon-blaze allures
The bird of passage, till he madly strikes
Against it and beats out his weary life.

For Philip's dwelling fronted on the street,
The latest house to landward; but behind,
With one small gate that open'd on the waste,
Flourish'd a little garden square and wall'd,
And in it throve an ancient evergreen,
A yew-tree, and all round it ran a walk
Of shingle, and a walk divided it.
But Enoch shunn'd the middle walk and stole
Up by the wall, behind the yew; and thence
That which he better might have shunn'd, if griefs
Like his have worse or better, Enoch saw.

For cups and silver on the burnish'd board
Sparkled and shone; so genial was the hearth;
And on the right hand of the hearth he saw
Philip, the slighted suitor of old times,
Stout, rosy, with his babe across his knees;
And o'er her second father stoopt a girl,
A later but a loftier Annie Lee,
Fair-hair'd and tall, and from her lifted hand
Dangled a length of ribbon and a ring
To tempt the babe, who rear'd his creasy arms,
Caught at and ever miss'd it, and they laugh'd;
And on the left hand of the hearth he saw
The mother glancing often toward her babe,
But turning now and then to speak with him,
Her son, who stood beside her tall and strong,
And saying that which pleased him, for he smiled.

Now when the dead man come to life beheld
His wife his wife no more, and saw the babe
Hers, yet not his, upon the father's knee,
And all the warmth, the peace, the happiness,
And his own children tall and beautiful,

And him, that other, reigning in his place,
Lord of his rights and of his children's love—
Then he, tho' Miriam Lane had told him all,
Because things seen are mightier than things heard,
Stagger'd and shook, holding the branch, and fear'd
To send abroad a shrill and terrible cry,
Which in one moment, like the blast of doom,
Would shatter all the happiness of the hearth.

He therefore turning softly like a thief,
Lest the harsh shingle should grate underfoot,
And feeling all along the garden-wall,
Lest he should swoon and tumble and be found,
Crept to the gate, and open'd it and closed,
As lightly as a sick man's chamber-door,
Behind him, and came out upon the waste.

And there he would have knelt, but that his knees
Were feeble, so that falling prone he dug
His fingers into the wet earth, and pray'd:

'Too hard to bear! why did they take me thence?
O God Almighty blessed Saviour, Thou
That didst uphold me on my lonely isle,
Uphold me, Father, in my loneliness
A little longer! aid me, give me strength
Not to tell her, never to let her know.
Help me not to break in upon her peace.
My children too! must I not speak to these?
They know me not. I should betray myself.
Never! no father's kiss for me—the girl
So like her mother, and the boy, my son.'

There speech and thought and nature fail'd a little,
And he lay tranced; but when he rose and paced
Back toward his solitary home again,
All down the long and narrow street he went
Beating it in upon his weary brain,
As tho' it were the burthen of a song,
'Not to tell her, never to let her know.'

He was not all unhappy. His resolve
Upbore him, and firm faith, and evermore
Prayer from a living source within the will,
And beating up thro' all the bitter world,
Like fountains of sweet water in the sea,
Kept him a living soul. 'This miller's wife,'
He said to Miriam, 'that you spoke about,
Has she no fear that her first husband lives?'
'Ay, ay, poor soul,' said Miriam, 'fear enow!
If you could tell her you had seen him dead,
Why, that would be her comfort;' and he thought,
'After the Lord has call'd me she shall know,
I wait His time;' and Enoch set himself,
Scorning an alms, to work whereby to live.
Almost to all things could he turn his hand.
Cooper he was and carpenter, and wrought
To make the boatmen fishing-nets, or help'd
At lading and unlading the tall barks
That brought the stinted commerce of those days,
Thus earn'd a scanty living for himself.
Yet since he did but labor for himself,
Work without hope, there was not life in it
Whereby the man could live; and as the year
Roll'd itself round again to meet the day
When Enoch had return'd, a languor came
Upon him, gentle sickness, gradually

Weakening the man, till he could do no more,
But kept the house, his chair, and last his bed.
And Enoch bore his weakness cheerfully.
For sure no gladlier does the stranded wreck
See thro' the gray skirts of a lifting squall
The boat that bears the hope of life approach
To save the life despair'd of, than he saw
Death dawning on him, and the close of all.

For thro' that dawning gleam'd a kindlier hope
On Enoch thinking, 'after I am gone,
Then may she learn I loved her to the last.'
He call'd aloud for Miriam Lane and said:
'Woman, I have a secret—only swear,
Before I tell you—swear upon the Book
Not to reveal it, till you see me dead.'
'Dead,' clamor'd the good woman, 'hear him talk!
I warrant, man, that we shall bring you round.'
'Swear,' added Enoch sternly, 'on the Book;'
And on the Book, half-frightened, Miriam swore.
Then Enoch rolling his gray eyes upon her,
'Did you know Enoch Arden of this town?'
'Know him?' she said, 'I knew him far away.
Ay, ay, I mind him coming down the street;
Held his head high, and cared for no man, he.'
Slowly and sadly Enoch answer'd her:
'His head is low, and no man cares for him.
I think I have not three days more to live;
I am the man.' At which the woman gave
A half-incredulous, half-hysterical cry:
'You Arden, you! nay,—sure he was a foot
Higher than you be.' Enoch said again:

'My God has bow'd me down to what I am;
My grief and solitude have broken me;
Nevertheless, know you that I am he
Who married—but that name has twice been changed—
I married her who married Philip Ray.
Sit, listen.' Then he told her of his voyage,
His wreck, his lonely life, his coming back,
His gazing in on Annie, his resolve,
And how he kept it. As the woman heard,
Fast flow'd the current of her easy tears,
While in her heart she yearn'd incessantly
To rush abroad all round the little haven,
Proclaiming Enoch Arden and his woes;
But awed and promise-bounden she forbore,
Saying only, 'See your bairns before you go!
Eh, let me fetch 'em, Arden,' and arose
Eager to bring them down, for Enoch hung
A moment on her words, but then replied:

'Woman, disturb me not now at the last,
But let me hold my purpose till I die.
Sit down again; mark me and understand,
While I have power to speak. I charge you now,
When you shall see her, tell her that I died
Blessing her, praying for her, loving her;
Save for the bar between us, loving her
As when she laid her head beside my own.
And tell my daughter Annie, whom I saw
So like her mother, that my latest breath
Was spent in blessing her and praying for her.
And tell my son that I died blessing him.
And say to Philip that I blest him too;

He never meant us anything but good.
But if my children care to see me dead,
Who hardly knew me living, let them come,
I am their father; but she must not come,
For my dead face would vex her after-life.
And now there is but one of all my blood
Who will embrace me in the world-to-be.
This hair is his, she cut it off and gave it,
And I have borne it with me all these years,
And thought to bear it with me to my grave;
But now my mind is changed, for I shall see him,
My babe in bliss. Wherefore when I am gone,
Take, give her this, for it may comfort her;
It will moreover be a token to her
That I am he.'

     He ceased; and Miriam Lane
Made such a voluble answer promising all,
That once again he roll'd his eyes upon her
Repeating all he wish'd, and once again
She promised.

     Then the third night after this,
While Enoch slumber'd motionless and pale,
And Miriam watch'd and dozed at intervals,
There came so loud a calling of the sea
That all the houses in the haven rang.
He woke, he rose, he spread his arms abroad,
Crying with a loud voice, 'A sail! a sail!
I am saved;' and so fell back and spoke no more.

 So past the strong heroic soul away.
And when they buried him the little port
Had seldom seen a costlier funeral.

THE PASSING OF ARTHUR

THAT story which the bold Sir Bedivere,
First made and latest left of all the knights,
Told, when the man was no more than a voice
In the white winter of his age, to those
With whom he dwelt, new faces, other minds.

For on their march to westward, Bedivere,
Who slowly paced among the slumbering host,
Heard in his tent the moanings of the King:

'I found Him in the shining of the stars,
I mark'd Him in the flowering of His fields,
But in His ways with men I find Him not.
I waged His wars, and now I pass and die.
O me! for why is all around us here
As if some lesser god had made the world,
But had not force to shape it as he would,
Till the High God behold it from beyond,
And enter it, and make it beautiful?
Or else as if the world were wholly fair,
But that these eyes of men are dense and dim,
And have not power to see it as it is—
Perchance, because we see not to the close;—
For I, being simple, thought to work His will,
And have but stricken with the sword in vain,
And all whereon I lean'd in wife and friend
Is traitor to my peace, and all my realm
Reels back into the beast, and is no more.
My God, thou hast forgotten me in my death!
Nay—God my Christ—I pass but shall not die.'

Then, ere that last weird battle in the west,
There came on Arthur sleeping, Gawain kill'd
In Lancelot's war, the ghost of Gawain blown
Along a wandering wind, and past his ear
Went shrilling: 'Hollow, hollow all delight!
Hail, King! to-morrow thou shalt pass away.
Farewell! there is an isle of rest for thee.
And I am blown along a wandering wind,
And hollow, hollow, hollow all delight!'
And fainter onward, like wild birds that change
Their season in the night and wail their way
From cloud to cloud, down the long wind the dream
Shrill'd; but in going mingled with dim cries
Far in the moonlit haze among the hills,
As of some lonely city sack'd by night,
When all is lost, and wife and child with wail
Pass to new lords; and Arthur woke and call'd:
'Who spake? A dream. O, light upon the wind,
Thine, Gawain, was the voice—are these dim cries
Thine? or doth all that haunts the waste and wild
Mourn, knowing it will go along with me?'

This heard the bold Sir Bedivere and spake:
'O me, my King, let pass whatever will,
Elves, and the harmless glamour of the field;
But in their stead thy name and glory cling
To all high places like a golden cloud
For ever; but as yet thou shalt not pass.
Light was Gawain in life, and light in death
Is Gawain, for the ghost is as the man;
And care not thou for dreams from him, but rise—
I hear the steps of Modred in the west,
And with him many of thy people, and knights
Once thine, whom thou hast loved, but grosser grown

Than heathen, spitting at their vows and thee.
Right well in heart they know thee for the King.
Arise, go forth and conquer as of old.'

Then spake King Arthur to Sir Bedivere:
'Far other is this battle in the west
Whereto we move than when we strove in youth,
And brake the petty kings, and fought with Rome,
Or thrust the heathen from the Roman wall,
And shook him thro' the north. Ill doom is mine
To war against my people and my knights.
The king who fights his people fights himself.
And they my knights, who loved me once, the stroke
That strikes them dead is as my death to me.
Yet let us hence, and find or feel a way
Thro' this blind haze which, ever since I saw
One lying in the dust at Almesbury,
Hath folded in the passes of the world.'

Then rose the King and moved his host by night,
And ever push'd Sir Modred, league by league,
Back to the sunset bound of Lyonnesse—
A land of old upheaven from the abyss
By fire, to sink into the abyss again;
Where fragments of forgotten peoples dwelt,
And the long mountains ended in a coast
Of ever-shifting sand, and far away
The phantom circle of a moaning sea.
There the pursuer could pursue no more,
And he that fled no further fly the King;
And there, that day when the great light of heaven
Burn'd at his lowest in the rolling year,
On the waste sand by the waste sea they closed.
Nor ever yet had Arthur fought a fight

Like this last, dim, weird battle of the west.
A death-white mist slept over sand and sea,
Whereof the chill, to him who breathed it, drew
Down with his blood, till all his heart was cold
With formless fear; and even on Arthur fell
Confusion, since he saw not whom he fought.
For friend and foe were shadows in the mist,
And friend slew friend not knowing whom he slew;
And some had visions out of golden youth,
And some beheld the faces of old ghosts
Look in upon the battle; and in the mist
Was many a noble deed, many a base,
And chance and craft and strength in single fights,
And ever and anon with host to host
Shocks, and the splintering spear, the hard mail hewn,
Shield-breakings, and the clash of brands, the crash
Of battle-axes on shatter'd helms, and shrieks
After the Christ, of those who falling down
Look'd up for heaven, and only saw the mist;
And shouts of heathen and the traitor knights,
Oaths, insult, filth, and monstrous blasphemies,
Sweat, writhings, anguish, laboring of the lungs
In that close mist, and cryings for the light,
Moans of the dying, and voices of the dead.

　　Last, as by some one death-bed after wail
Of suffering, silence follows, or thro' death
Or death-like swoon, thus over all that shore,
Save for some whisper of the seething seas,
A dead hush fell; but when the dolorous day
Grew drearier toward twilight falling, came
A bitter wind, clear from the north, and blew
The mist aside, and with that wind the tide
Rose, and the pale King glanced across the field

Of battle. But no man was moving there;
Nor any cry of Christian heard thereon,
Nor yet of heathen; only the wan wave
Brake in among dead faces, to and fro
Swaying the helpless hands, and up and down
Tumbling the hollow helmets of the fallen,
And shiver'd brands that once had fought with Rome,
And rolling far along the gloomy shores
The voice of days of old and days to be.

Then spake King Arthur to Sir Bedivere,
And whiter than the mist that all day long
Had held the field of battle was the King:

'Hearest thou this great voice that shakes the world,
And wastes the narrow realm whereon we move,
And beats upon the faces of the dead,
My dead, as tho' they had not died for me?—
O Bedivere, for on my heart hath fallen
Confusion, till I know not what I am,
Nor whence I am, nor whether I be king;
Behold, I seem but king among the dead.'

Then spake the bold Sir Bedivere: 'My King!
King everywhere! and so the dead have kings,
There also will I worship thee as king.
Yet still thy life is whole, and still I live
Who love thee; but who hates thee, he that brought
The heathen back among us, yonder stands,
Modred, unharm'd, the traitor of thine house.'

Then spake the King: 'My house hath been my doom.
But call not thou this traitor of my house
Who hath but dwelt beneath one roof with me.

My house are rather they who sware my vows,
Yea, even while they brake them, own'd me king.
And well for thee, saying in my dark hour,
When all the purport of my throne hath fail'd,
That quick or dead thou holdest me for king.
King am I, whatsoever be their cry;
And one last act of kinghood shalt thou see
Yet, ere I pass.' And uttering this the King
Made at the man. Then Modred smote his liege
Hard on that helm which many a heathen sword
Had beaten thin; while Arthur at one blow,
Striking the last stroke with Excalibur,
Slew him, and, all but slain himself, he fell.

So all day long the noise of battle roll'd
Among the mountains by the winter sea,
Until King Arthur's Table, man by man,
Had fallen in Lyonnesse about their lord,
King Arthur; then, because his wound was deep,
The bold Sir Bedivere uplifted him,
And bore him to a chapel nigh the field,
A broken chancel with a broken cross,
That stood on a dark strait of barren land.
On one side lay the Ocean, and on one
Lay a great water, and the moon was full.

Then spake King Arthur to Sir Bedivere:
'The sequel of to-day unsolders all
The goodliest fellowship of famous knights
Whereof this world holds record. Such a sleep
They sleep—the men I loved. I think that we
Shall never more, at any future time,
Delight our souls with talk of knightly deeds,
Walking about the gardens and the halls

Of Camelot, as in the days that were.
I perish by this people which I made,—
Tho' Merlin sware that I should come again
To rule once more—but let what will be be,
I am so deeply smitten thro' the helm
That without help I cannot last till morn.
Thou therefore take my brand Excalibur,
Which was my pride; for thou rememberest **how**
In those old days, one summer noon, an arm
Rose up from out the bosom of the lake,
Clothed in white samite, mystic, wonderful,
Holding the sword—and how I row'd across
And took it, and have worn it, like a king;
And, wheresoever I am sung or told
In aftertime, this also shall be known.
But now delay not; take Excalibur,
And fling him far into the middle mere;
Watch what thou seest, and lightly bring me **word.'**

To him replied the bold Sir Bedivere:
'It is not meet, Sir King, to leave thee thus,
Aidless, alone, and smitten thro' the helm—
A little thing may harm a wounded man;
Yet I thy hest will all perform at full,
Watch what I see, and lightly bring thee word.'

So saying, from the ruin'd shrine he stept,
And in the moon athwart the place of tombs,
Where lay the mighty bones of ancient men,
Old knights, and over them the seawind sang
Shrill, chill, with flakes of foam. He, stepping **down**
By zigzag paths and juts of pointed rock,
Came on the shining levels of the lake.

There drew he forth the brand Excalibur,
And o'er him, drawing it, the winter moon,
Brightening the skirts of a long cloud, ran forth
And sparkled keen with frost against the hilt;
For all the haft twinkled with diamond sparks,
Myriads of topaz-lights, and jacinth-work
Of subtlest jewellery. He gazed so long
That both his eyes were dazzled as he stood,
This way and that dividing the swift mind,
In act to throw; but at the last it seem'd
Better to leave Excalibur conceal'd
There in the many-knotted water-flags,
That whistled stiff and dry about the marge.
So strode he back slow to the wounded King.

Then spake King Arthur to Sir Bedivere:
'Hast thou perform'd my mission which I gave?
What is it thou hast seen? or what hast heard?'

And answer made the bold Sir Bedivere:
'I heard the ripple washing in the reeds,
And the wild water lapping on the crag.'

To whom replied King Arthur, faint and pale:
'Thou hast betray'd thy nature and thy name,
Not rendering true answer, as beseem'd
Thy fealty, nor like a noble knight;
For surer sign had follow'd, either hand,
Or voice, or else a motion of the mere.
This is a shameful thing for men to lie.
Yet now, I charge thee, quickly go again,
As thou art lief and dear, and do the thing
I bade thee, watch, and lightly bring me word.'

Then went Sir Bedivere the second time
Across the ridge, and paced beside the mere,
Counting the dewy pebbles, fixt in thought;
But when he saw the wonder of the hilt,
How curiously and strangely chased, he smote
His palms together, and he cried aloud:

'And if indeed I cast the brand away,
Surely a precious thing, one worthy note,
Should thus be lost for ever from the earth,
Which might have pleased the eyes of many men.
What good should follow this, if this were done?
What harm, undone? Deep harm to disobey,
Seeing obedience is the bond of rule.
Were it well to obey then, if a king demand
An act unprofitable, against himself?
The King is sick, and knows not what he does.
What record or what relic of my lord
Should be to aftertime, but empty breath
And rumors of a doubt? But were this kept,
Stored in some treasure-house of mighty kings,
Some one might show it at a joust of arms,
Saying: "King Arthur's sword, Excalibur,
Wrought by the lonely Maiden of the Lake.
Nine years she wrought it, sitting in the deeps
Upon the hidden bases of the hills."
So might some old man speak in the aftertime
To all the people, winning reverence.
But now much honor and much fame were lost.'

So spake he, clouded with his own conceit,
And hid Excalibur the second time,
And so strode back slow to the wounded King.

Then spoke King Arthur, breathing heavily:
'What is it thou hast seen? or what hast heard?'

And answer made the bold Sir Bedivere:
'I heard the water lapping on the crag,
And the long ripple washing in the reeds.'

To whom replied King Arthur, much in wrath:
'Ah miserable, and unkind, untrue,
Unknightly, traitor-hearted! Woe is me!
Authority forgets a dying king,
Laid widow'd of the power in his eye
That bow'd the will. I see thee what thou art,
For thou, the latest-left of all my knights,
In whom should meet the offices of all,
Thou wouldst betray me for the precious hilt;
Either from lust of gold, or like a girl
Valuing the giddy pleasure of the eyes.
Yet, for a man may fail in duty twice,
And the third time may prosper, get thee hence;
But, if thou spare to fling Excalibur,
I will arise and slay thee with my hands.'

Then quickly rose Sir Bedivere, and ran,
And, leaping down the ridges lightly, plunged
Among the bulrush beds, and clutch'd the sword,
And strongly wheel'd and threw it. The great brand
Made lightnings in the splendor of the moon,
And flashing round and round, and whirl'd in an arch,
Shot like a streamer of the northern morn,
Seen where the moving isles of winter shock
By night, with noises of the Northern Sea.
So flash'd and fell the brand Excalibur;
But ere he dipt the surface, rose an arm

Clothed in white samite, mystic, wonderful,
And caught him by the hilt, and brandish'd him
Three times, and drew him under in the mere.
And lightly went the other to the King.

Then spoke King Arthur, drawing thicker breath:
'Now see I by thine eyes that this is done.
Speak out; what is it thou hast heard, or seen?'

And answer made the bold Sir Bedivere:
'Sir King, I closed mine eyelids, lest the gems
Should blind my purpose, for I never saw,
Nor shall see, here or elsewhere, till I die,
Not tho' I live three lives of mortal men,
So great a miracle as yonder hilt.
Then with both hands I flung him, wheeling him;
But when I look'd again, behold an arm,
Clothed in white samite, mystic, wonderful,
That caught him by the hilt, and brandish'd him
Three times, and drew him under in the mere.'

And answer made King Arthur, breathing hard:
'My ends draws nigh; 't is time that I were gone.
Make broad thy shoulders to receive my weight,
And bear me to the margin; yet I fear
My wound hath taken cold, and I shall die.'

So saying, from the pavement he half rose,
Slowly, with pain, reclining on his arm,
And looking wistfully with wide blue eyes
As in a picture. Him Sir Bedivere
Remorsefully regarded thro' his tears,
And would have spoken, but he found not words;
Then took with care, and kneeling on one knee,

O'er both his shoulders drew the languid hands,
And rising bore him thro' the place of tombs.

  But, as he walk'd, King Arthur panted hard,
Like one that feels a nightmare on his bed
When all the house is mute. So sigh'd the King,
Muttering and murmuring at his ear, 'Quick, quick!
I fear it is too late, and I shall die.'
But the other swiftly strode from ridge to ridge,
Clothed with his breath, and looking, as he walk'd,
Larger than human on the frozen hills.
He heard the deep behind him, and a cry
Before. His own thought drove him like a goad.
Dry clash'd his harness in the icy caves
And barren chasms, and all to left and right
The bare black cliff clang'd round him, as he based
His feet on juts of slippery crag that rang
Sharp-smitten with the dint of armed heels—
And on a sudden, lo, the level lake,
And the long glories of the winter moon!

  Then saw they how there hove a dusky barge,
Dark as a funeral scarf from stem to stern,
Beneath them; and descending they were ware
That all the decks were dense with stately forms,
Black-stoled, black-hooded, like a dream—by these
Three queens with crowns of gold—and from them rose
A cry that shiver'd to the tingling stars,
And, as it were one voice, an agony
Of lamentation, like a wind that shrills
All night in a waste land, where no one comes,
Or hath come, since the making of the world.

  Then murmur'd Arthur, 'Place me in the barge.'
So to the barge they came. There those three queens

Put forth their hands, and took the King, and wept.
But she that rose the tallest of them all
And fairest laid his head upon her lap,
And loosed the shatter'd casque, and chafed his hands,
And call'd him by his name, complaining loud,
And dropping bitter tears against a brow
Striped with dark blood; for all his face was white
And colorless, and like the wither'd moon
Smote by the fresh beam of the springing east;
And all his greaves and cuisses dash'd with drops
Of onset; and the light and lustrous curls—
That made his forehead like a rising sun
High from the dais-throne—were parch'd with dust,
Or, clotted into points and hanging loose,
Mixt with the knightly growth that fringed his lips.
So like a shatter'd column lay the King;
Not like that Arthur who, with lance in rest,
From spur to plume a star of tournament,
Shot thro' the lists at Camelot, and charged
Before the eyes of ladies and of kings.

  Then loudly cried the bold Sir Bedivere:
'Ah! my Lord Arthur, whither shall I go?
Where shall I hide my forehead and my eyes?
For now I see the true old times are dead,
When every morning brought a noble chance,
And every chance brought out a noble knight.
Such times have been not since the light that led
The holy Elders with the gift of myrrh.
But now the whole Round Table is dissolved
Which was an image of the mighty world;
And I, the last, go forth companionless,
And the days darken round me, and the years,
Among new men, strange faces, other minds.'

And slowly answer'd Arthur from the barge:
'The old order changeth, yielding place to new,
And God fulfils himself in many ways,
Lest one good custom should corrupt the world.
Comfort thyself; what comfort is in me?
I have lived my life, and that which I have done
May He within himself make pure! but thou,
If thou shouldst never see my face again,
Pray for my soul. More things are wrought by prayer
Than this world dreams of. Wherefore, let thy voice
Rise like a fountain for me night and day.
For what are men better than sheep or goats
That nourish a blind life within the brain,
If, knowing God, they lift not hands of prayer
Both for themselves and those who call them friend?
For so the whole round earth is every way
Bound by gold chains about the feet of God.
But now farewell. I am going a long way
With these thou seest—if indeed I go—
For all my mind is clouded with a doubt—
To the island-valley of Avilion;
Where falls not hail, or rain, or any snow,
Nor ever wind blows loudly; but it lies
Deep-meadow'd, happy, fair with orchard lawns
And bowery hollows crown'd with summer sea,
Where I will heal me of my grievous wound.'

So said he, and the barge with oar and sail
Moved from the brink, like some full-breasted swan
That, fluting a wild carol ere her death,
Ruffles her pure cold plume, and takes the flood
With swarthy webs. Long stood Sir Bedivere
Revolving many memories, till the hull

Look'd one black dot against the verge of dawn,
And on the mere the wailing died away.

But when that moan had past for evermore,
The stillness of the dead world's winter dawn
Amazed him, and he groan'd, 'The King is gone.'
And therewithal came on him the weird rhyme,
'From the great deep to the great deep he goes.'

Whereat he slowly turn'd and slowly clomb
The last hard footstep of that iron crag,
Thence mark'd the black hull moving yet, and cried:
'He passes to be king among the dead,
And after healing of his grievous wound
He comes again; but—if he come no more—
O me, be yon dark queens in yon black boat,
Who shriek'd and wail'd, the three whereat we gazed
On that high day, when, clothed with living light,
They stood before his throne in silence, friends
Of Arthur, who should help him at his need?'

Then from the dawn it seem'd there came, but faint
As from beyond the limit of the world,
Like the last echo born of a great cry,
Sounds, as if some fair city were one voice
Around a king returning from his wars.

Thereat once more he moved about, and clomb
Even to the highest he could climb, and saw,
Straining his eyes beneath an arch of hand,
Or thought he saw, the speck that bare the King,
Down that long water opening on the deep
Somewhere far off, pass on and on, and go
From less to less and vanish into light.
And the new sun rose bringing the new year.

ALLEGORIES

THE PALACE OF ART

TO R. C. TRENCH

I SEND you here a sort of allegory—
For you will understand it—of a soul,
A sinful soul possess'd of many gifts,
A spacious garden full of flowering weeds,
A glorious devil, large in heart and brain,
That did love beauty only—beauty seen
In all varieties of mould and mind—
And knowledge for its beauty; or if good,
Good only for its beauty, seeing not
That Beauty, Good, and Knowledge are three sisters
That dote upon each other, friends to man,
Living together under the same roof,
And never can be sunder'd without tears.
And he that shuts Love out, in turn shall be
Shut out from Love, and on her threshold lie
Howling in outer darkness. Not for this
Was common clay ta'en from the common earth
Moulded by God, and temper'd with the tears
Of angels to the perfect shape of man.

I built my soul a lordly pleasure house,
   Wherein at ease for aye to dwell.
I said, 'O Soul, make merry and carouse,
     Dear soul, for all is well.'

A huge crag-platform, smooth as burnish'd brass,
  I chose. The ranged ramparts bright
From level meadow-bases of deep grass
    Suddenly scaled the light.

Thereon I built it firm. Of ledge or shelf
  The rock rose clear, or winding stair.
My soul would live alone unto herself
    In her high palace there.

And 'while the world runs round and round,' I said,
  'Reign thou apart, a quiet king,
Still as, while Saturn whirls, his steadfast shade
    Sleeps on his luminous ring.'

To which my soul made answer readily:
  'Trust me, in bliss I shall abide
In this great mansion, that is built for me,
    So royal-rich and wide.'

        .   .   .   .

Four courts I made, East, West and South and North,
  In each a squared lawn, wherefrom
The golden gorge of dragons spouted forth
    A flood of fountain-foam.

And round the cool green courts there ran a row
  Of cloisters, branch'd like mighty woods,
Echoing all night to that sonorous flow
    Of spouted fountain-floods;

And round the roofs a gilded gallery
  That lent broad verge to distant lands,
Far as the wild swan wings, to where the sky
    Dipt down to sea and sands.

From those four jets four currents in one swell
   Across the mountain stream'd below
In misty folds, that floating as they fell
    Lit up a torrent-bow.

And high on every peak a statue seem'd
   To hang on tiptoe, tossing up
A cloud of incense of all odor steam'd
    From out a golden cup.

So that she thought, 'And who shall gaze upon
   My palace with unblinded eyes,
While this great bow will waver in the sun,
    And that sweet incense rise?'

For that sweet incense rose and never fail'd,
   And, while day sank or mounted higher,
The light aerial gallery, golden-rail'd,
    Burnt like a fringe of fire.

Likewise the deep-set windows, stain'd and traced,
   Would seem slow-flaming crimson fires
From shadow'd grots of arches interlaced,
    And tipt with frost-like spires.

.   .   .   .

Full of long-sounding corridors it was,
   That over-vaulted grateful gloom,
Thro' which the livelong day my soul did pass,
    Well-pleased, from room to room.

Full of great rooms and small the palace stood,
   All various, each a perfect whole
From living Nature, fit for every mood
    And change of my still soul.

For some were hung with arras green and blue,
　　Showing a gaudy summer-morn,
Where with puff'd cheek the belted hunter blew
　　His wreathed bugle-horn.

One seem'd all dark and red—a tract of sand,
　　And some one pacing there alone,
Who paced for ever in a glimmering land,
　　Lit with a low large moon.

One show'd an iron coast and angry waves.
　　You seem'd to hear them climb and fall
And roar rock-thwarted under bellowing caves,
　　Beneath the windy wall.

And one, a full-fed river winding slow
　　By herds upon an endless plain,
The ragged rims of thunder brooding low,
　　With shadow-streaks of rain.

And one, the reapers at their sultry toil.
　　In front they bound the sheaves. Behind
Were realms of upland, prodigal in oil,
　　And hoary to the wind.

And one a foreground black with stones and slags;
　　Beyond, a line of heights; and higher
All barr'd with long white cloud the scornful crags;
　　And highest, snow and fire.

And one, an English home—gray twilight pour'd
　　On dewy pastures, dewy trees,
Softer than sleep—all things in order stored,
　　A haunt of ancient Peace.

Nor these alone, but every landscape fair,
  As fit for every mood of mind,
Or gay, or grave, or sweet, or stern, was there,
  Not less than truth design'd.

        .   .   .   .

Or the maid-mother by a crucifix,
  In tracts of pasture sunny-warm,
Beneath branch-work of costly sardonyx
  Sat smiling, babe in arm.

Or in a clear-wall'd city on the sea,
  Near gilded organ-pipes, her' hair
Wound with white roses, slept Saint Cecily;
  An angel look'd at her.

Or thronging all one porch of Paradise
  A group of Houris bow'd to see
The dying Islamite, with hands and eyes
  That said, We wait for thee.

Or mythic Uther's deeply-wounded son
  In some fair space of sloping greens
Lay, dozing in the vale of Avalon,
  And watch'd by weeping queens.

Or hollowing one hand against his ear,
  To list a foot-fall, ere he saw
The wood-nymph, stay'd the Ausonian king to hear
  Of wisdom and of law.

Or over hills with peaky tops engrail'd,
  And many a tract of palm and rice,
The throne of Indian Cama slowly sail'd
  A summer fann'd with spice.

Or sweet Europa's mantle blew unclasp'd,
　From off her shoulder backward borne;
From one hand droop'd a crocus; one hand grasp'd
　　The mild bull's golden horn.

Or else flush'd Ganymede, his rosy thigh
　Half-buried in the eagle's down,
Sole as a flying star shot thro' the sky
　　Above the pillar'd town.

Nor these alone; but every legend fair
　Which the supreme Caucasian mind
Carved out of Nature for itself was there,
　　Not less than life design'd.

　　　　·　·　·　·　·　·　·

Then in the towers I placed great bells that swung,
　Moved of themselves, with silver sound;
And with choice paintings of wise men I hung
　　The royal dais round.

For there was Milton like a seraph strong,
　Beside him Shakespeare bland and mild;
And there the world-worn Dante grasp'd his song,
　　And somewhat grimly smiled.

And there the Ionian father of the rest;
　A million wrinkles carved his skin;
A hundred winters snow'd upon his breast,
　　From cheek and throat and chin.

Above, the fair hall-ceiling stately-set
　Many an arch high up did lift,
And angels rising and descending met
　　With interchange of gift.

Below was all mosaic choicely plann'd
    With cycles of the human tale
Of this wide world, the times of every land
    So wrought they will not fail.

The people here, a beast of burden slow,
    Toil'd onward, prick'd with goads and stings;
Here play'd, a tiger, rolling to and fro
    The heads and crowns of kings;

Here rose, an athlete, strong to break or bind
    All force in bonds that might endure,
And here once more like some sick man declined,
    And trusted any cure.

But over these she trod; and those great bells
    Began to chime. She took her throne;
She sat betwixt the shining oriels,
    To sing her songs alone.

And thro' the topmost oriels' colored flame
    Two godlike faces gazed below;
Plato the wise, and large-brow'd Verulam,
    The first of those who know.

And all those names that in their motion were
    Full-welling fountain-heads of change,
Betwixt the slender shafts were blazon'd fair
    In diverse raiment strange;

Thro' which the lights, rose, amber, emerald, blue,
    Flush'd in her temples and her eyes,
And from her lips, as morn from Memnon, drew
    Rivers of melodies.

No nightingale delighteth to prolong
  Her low preamble all alone,
More than my soul to hear her echo'd song
    Throb thro' the ribbed stone;

Singing and murmuring in her feastful mirth,
  Joying to feel herself alive,
Lord over Nature, lord of the visible earth,
    Lord of the senses five;

Communing with herself: 'All these are mine,
  And let the world have peace or wars,
'T is one to me.' She—when young night divine
    Crown'd dying day with stars,

Making sweet close of his delicious toils—
  Lit light in wreaths and anadems,
And pure quintessences of precious oils
    In hollow'd moons of gems,

To mimic heaven; and clapt her hands and cried,
  'I marvel if my still delight
In this great house so royal-rich and wide
    Be flatter'd to the height.

'O all things fair to sate my various eyes!
  O shapes and hues that please me well!
O silent faces of the Great and Wise,
    My Gods, with whom I dwell!

'O Godlike isolation which art mine,
  I can but count thee perfect gain,
What time I watch the darkening droves of swine
    That range on yonder plain.

'In filthy sloughs they roll a prurient skin,
    They graze and wallow, breed and sleep;
And oft some brainless devil enters in,
        And drives them to the deep.'

Then of the moral instinct would she prate
    And of the rising from the dead,
As hers by right of full-accomplish'd Fate;
        And at the last she said:

'I take possession of man's mind and deed.
    I care not what the sects may brawl.
I sit as God holding no form of creed,
        But contemplating all.'

        .   .   .   .

Full oft the riddle of the painful earth
    Flash'd thro' her as she sat alone,
Yet not the less held she her solemn mirth,
        And intellectual throne.

And so she throve and prosper'd; so three years
    She prosper'd; on the fourth she fell,
Like Herod, when the shout was in his ears,
        Struck thro' with pangs of hell.

Lest she should fail and perish utterly,
    God, before whom ever lie bare
The abysmal deeps of personality,
        Plagued her with sore despair.

When she would think, where'er she turn'd her sight
    The airy hand confusion wrought,
Wrote, 'Mene, mene,' and divided quite
        The kingdom of her thought.

Deep dread and loathing of her solitude
　Fell on her, from which mood was born
Scorn of herself; again, from out that mood
　　Laughter at her self-scorn.

'What! is not this my place of strength,' she said,
　'My spacious mansion built for me,
Whereof the strong foundation-stones were laid
　　Since my first memory?'

But in dark corners of her palace stood
　Uncertain shapes; and unawares
On white-eyed phantasms weeping tears of blood,
　　And horrible nightmares,

And hollow shades enclosing hearts of flame,
　And, with dim fretted foreheads all,
On corpses three-months-old at noon she came,
　　That stood against the wall.

A spot of dull stagnation, without light
　Or power of movement, seem'd my soul,
Mid onward-sloping motions infinite
　　Making for one sure goal;

A still salt pool, lock'd in with bars of sand,
　Left on the shore, that hears all night
The plunging seas draw backward from the land
　　Their moon-led waters white;

A star that with the choral starry dance
　Join'd not, but stood, and standing saw
The hollow orb of moving Circumstance
　　Roll'd round by one fix'd law.

Back on herself her serpent pride had curl'd.
   'No voice,' she shriek'd in that lone hall,
'No voice breaks thro' the stillness of this world;
     One deep, deep silence all!'

She, mouldering with the dull earth's mouldering sod,
   Inwrapt tenfold in slothful shame,
Lay there exiled from eternal God,
     Lost to her place and name:

And death and life she hated equally,
   And nothing saw, for her despair,
But dreadful time, dreadful eternity,
     No comfort anywhere;

Remaining utterly confused with fears,
   And ever worse with growing time,
And ever unrelieved by dismal tears,
     And all alone in crime.

Shut up as in a crumbling tomb, girt round
   With blackness as a solid wall,
Far off she seem'd to hear the dully sound
     Of human footsteps fall:

As in strange lands a traveller walking slow,
   In doubt and great perplexity,
A little before moonrise hears the low
     Moan of an unknown sea;

And knows not if it be thunder, or a sound
   Of rocks thrown down, or one deep cry
Of great wild beasts; then thinketh,
     'I have found
     A new land, but I die.'

She howl'd aloud, 'I am on fire within.
  There comes no murmur of reply.
What is it that will take away my sin,
    And save me lest I die?'

So when four years were wholly finished,
  She threw her royal robes away.
'Make me a cottage in the vale,' she said,
    'Where I may mourn and pray.

'Yet pull not down my palace towers, that are
  So lightly, beautifully built;
Perchance I may return with others there
    When I have purged my guilt.'

THE VISION OF SIN

I HAD a vision when the night was late;
A youth came riding toward a palace-gate.
He rode a horse with wings, that would have flown,
But that his heavy rider kept him down.
And from the palace came a child of sin,
And took him by the curls, and led him in,
Where sat a company with heated eyes,
Expecting when a fountain should arise.
A sleepy light upon their brows and lips—
As when the sun, a crescent of eclipse,
Dreams over lake and lawn, and isles and capes—
Suffused them, sitting, lying, languid shapes,
By heaps of gourds, and skins of wine,
    and piles of grapes.

Then methought I heard a mellow sound,
Gathering up from all the lower ground;
Narrowing in to where they sat assembled,
Low voluptuous music winding trembled,
Woven in circles. They that heard it sigh'd,
Panted hand-in-hand with faces pale,
Swung themselves, and in low tones replied;
Till the fountain spouted, showering wide
Sleet of diamond-drift and pearly hail.
Then the music touch'd the gates and died,
Rose again from where it seem'd to fail,
Storm'd in orbs of song, a growing gale;
Till thronging in and in, to where they waited,
As 't were a hundred-throated nightingale,
The strong tempestuous treble throbb'd and palpitated;
Ran into its giddiest whirl of sound,
Caught the sparkles, and in circles,
Purple gauzes, golden hazes, liquid mazes,
Flung the torrent rainbow round.
Then they started from their places,
Moved with violence, changed in hue,
Caught each other with wild grimaces,
Half-invisible to the view,
Wheeling with precipitate paces
To the melody, till they flew,
Hair and eyes and limbs and faces,
Twisted hard in fierce embraces,
Like to Furies, like to Graces,
Dash'd together in blinding dew;
Till, kill'd with some luxurious agony,
The nerve-dissolving melody
Flutter'd headlong from the sky.

And then I look'd up toward a mountain-tract,
That girt the region with high cliff and lawn.

I saw that every morning, far withdrawn
Beyond the darkness and the cataract,
God made Himself an awful rose of dawn,
Unheeded; and detaching, fold by fold,
From those still heights, and, slowly drawing near,
A vapor heavy, hueless, formless, cold,
Came floating on for many a month and year,
Unheeded; and I thought I would have spoken,
And warn'd that madman ere it grew too late,
But, as in dreams, I could not. Mine was broken,
When that cold vapor touch'd the palace-gate,
And link'd again. I saw within my head
A gray and tap-tooth'd man as lean as death,
Who slowly rode across a wither'd heath,
And lighted at a ruin'd inn, and said:

'Wrinkled ostler, grim and thin!
  Here is custom come your way;
Take my brute, and lead him in,
  Stuff his ribs with mouldy hay.

'Bitter barmaid, waning fast!
  See that sheets are on my bed.
What! the flower of life is past;
  It is long before you wed.

'Slip-shod waiter, lank and sour,
  At the Dragon on the heath!
Let us have a quiet hour,
  Let us hob-and-nob with Death.

'I am old, but let me drink;
  Bring me spices, bring me wine;
I remember, when I think,
  That my youth was half divine.

'Wine is good for shrivell'd lips,
    When a blanket wraps the day,
When the rotten woodland drips,
    And the leaf is stamp'd in clay.

'Sit thee down, and have no shame,
    Cheek by jowl, and knee by knee;
What care I for any name?
    What for order or degree?

'Let me screw thee up a peg;
    Let me loose thy tongue with wine;
Callest thou that thing a leg?
    Which is thinnest? thine or mine?

'Thou shalt not be saved by works,
    Thou hast been a sinner too;
Ruin'd trunks on wither'd forks,
    Empty scarecrows, I and you!

'Fill the cup and fill the can,
    Have a rouse before the morn;
Every moment dies a man,
    Every moment one is born.

'We are men of ruin'd blood;
    Therefore comes it we are wise.
Fish are we that love the mud,
    Rising to no fancy-flies.

'Name and fame! to fly sublime
    Thro' the courts, the camps, the schools,
Is to be the ball of Time,
    Bandied by the hands of fools.

'Friendship!—to be two in one—
  Let the canting liar pack!
Well I know, when I am gone,
  How she mouths behind my back.

'Virtue!—to be good and just—
  Every heart, when sifted well,
Is a clot of warmer dust,
  Mix'd with cunning sparks of hell.

'O we two as well can look
  Whited thought and cleanly life
As the priest, above his book
  Leering at his neighbor's wife.

'Fill the cup and fill the can,
  Have a rouse before the morn:
Every moment dies a man,
  Every moment one is born.

'Drink, and let the parties rave;
  They are fill'd with idle spleen,
Rising, falling, like a wave,
  For they know not what they mean.

'He that roars for liberty
  Faster binds a tyrant's power,
And the tyrant's cruel glee
  Forces on the freer hour.

'Fill the can and fill the cup;
  All the windy ways of men
Are but dust that rises up,
  And is lightly laid again.

'Greet her with applausive breath,
  Freedom, gaily doth she tread;
In her right a civic wreath,
  In her left a human head.

'No, I love not what is new;
  She is of an ancient house,
And I think we know the hue
  Of that cap upon her brows.

'Let her go! her thirst she slakes
  Where the bloody conduit runs,
Then her sweetest meal she makes
  On the first-born of her sons.

'Drink to lofty hopes that cool,—
  Visions of a perfect State;
Drink we, last, the public fool,
  Frantic love and frantic hate.

'Chant me now some wicked stave
  Till thy drooping courage rise,
And the glow-worm of the grave
  Glimmer in thy rheumy eyes.

'Fear not thou to loose thy tongue,
  Set thy hoary fancies free;
What is loathsome to the young
  Savors well to thee and me.

'Change, reverting to the years,
  When thy nerves could understand
What there is in loving tears,
  And the warmth of hand in hand.

'Tell me tales of thy first love—
    April hopes, the fools of chance—
Till the graves begin to move,
    And the dead begin to dance.

'Fill the can and fill the cup;
All the windy ways of men
Are but dust that rises up,
    And is lightly laid again.

'Trooping from their mouldy dens
    The chap-fallen circle spreads—
Welcome, fellow-citizens,
    Hollow hearts and empty heads!

'You are bones, and what of that?
    Every face, however full,
Padded round with flesh and fat,
    Is but modell'd on a skull.

'Death is king, and Vivat Rex!
    Tread a measure on the stones,
Madam—if I know your sex
    From the fashion of your bones.

'No, I cannot praise the fire
    In your eye—nor yet your lip;
All the more do I admire
    Joints of cunning workmanship.

'Lo! God's likeness—the ground-plan—
    Neither modell'd, glazed, nor framed;
Buss me, thou rough sketch of man,
    Far too naked to be shamed!

'Drink to Fortune, drink to Chance,
    While we keep a little breath!

Drink to heavy Ignorance!
  Hob-and-nob with brother Death!

'Thou art mazed, the night is long,
  And the longer night is near—
What! I am not all as wrong
  As a bitter jest is dear.

'Youthful hopes, by scores, to all,
  When the locks are crisp and curl'd;
Unto me my maudlin gall
  And my mockeries of the world.

'Fill the cup and fill the can;
  Mingle madness, mingle scorn!
Dregs of life, and lees of man;
  Yet we will not die forlorn.'

The voice grew faint; there came a further change;
Once more uprose the mystic mountain-range.
Below were men and horses pierced with worms,
And slowly quickening into lower forms,
By shards and scurf of salt, and scum of dross,
Old plash of rains, and refuse patch'd with moss.
Then some one spake: 'Behold! it was a crime
Of sense avenged by sense that wore with time.'
Another said: 'The crime of sense became
The crime of malice, and is equal blame.'
And one: 'He had not wholly quench'd his power;
A little grain of conscience made him sour.'
At last I heard a voice upon the slope
Cry to the summit, 'Is there any hope?'
To which an answer peal'd from that high land,
But in a tongue no man could understand;
And on the glimmering limit far withdrawn
God made Himself an awful rose of dawn.

TO POETS

MILTON

O MIGHTY-MOUTH'D inventor of harmonies,
O skill'd to sing of Time or Eternity,
  God-gifted organ-voice of England,
    Milton, a name to resound for ages;
Whose Titan angels, Gabriel, Abdiel,
Starr'd from Jehovah's gorgeous armories,
  Tower, as the deep-domed empyrean
    Rings to the roar of an angel onset!
Me rather all that bowery loneliness,
The brooks of Eden mazily murmuring,
  And bloom profuse and cedar arches
    Charm, as a wanderer out in ocean,
Where some refulgent sunset of India
Streams o'er a rich ambrosial ocean isle,
  And crimson-hued the stately palm-woods
    Whisper in odorous heights of even.

DANTE

(WRITTEN AT REQUEST OF THE FLORENTINES)

KING, that hast reign'd six hundred years, and grown
In power, and ever growest, since thine own
Fair Florence honoring thy nativity,
Thy Florence now the crown of Italy.
Hath sought the tribute of a verse from me,
I, wearing but the garland of a day,
Cast at thy feet one flower that fades away.

VIRGIL

WRITTEN AT THE REQUEST OF THE MANTUANS FOR THE NINE-
TEENTH CENTENARY OF VIRGIL'S DEATH

ROMAN VIRGIL, thou that singest Ilion's lofty temples robed
    in fire,
Ilion falling, Rome arising, wars, and filial faith, and Dido's
    pyre;

Landscape-lover, lord of language more than he that sang the
    'Works and Days,'
All the chosen coin of fancy flashing out from many a golden
    phrase;

Thou that singest wheat and woodland, tilth and vineyard,
    hive and horse and herd;
All the charm of all the Muses often flowering in a lonely
    word;

Poet of the happy Tityrus piping underneath his beechen
    bowers;
Poet of the poet-satyr whom the laughing shepherd bound
    with flowers;

Chanter of the Pollio, glorying in the blissful years again
    to be,
Summers of the snakeless meadow, unlaborious earth and
    oarless sea;

Thou that seest Universal Nature moved by Universal Mind;
Thou majestic in thy sadness at the doubtful doom of human
    kind;

Light among the vanish'd ages; star that gildest yet this
    phantom shore;
Golden branch amid the shadows, kings and realms that pass
    to rise no more;

Now thy Forum roars no longer, fallen every purple Cæsar's
    dome—
Tho' thine ocean-roll of rhythm sound forever of Imperial
    Rome—

Now the Rome of slaves hath perish'd, and the Rome of
    freemen holds her place,
I, from out the Northern Island sunder'd once from all the
    human race,

I salute thee, Mantovano, I that loved thee since my day
    began,
Wielder of the stateliest measure ever moulded by the lips
    of man.

CATULLUS

Row us out from Desenzano, to your Sirmione row!
So they row'd, and there we landed—'O venusta Sirmio!'
There to me thro' all the groves of olive in the summer glow,
There beneath the Roman ruin where the purple flowers grow,
Came that 'Ave atque Vale' of the Poet's hopeless woe,
Tenderest of Roman poets nineteen hundred years ago,
'Frater Ave atque Vale'—as we wander'd to and fro
Gazing at the Lydian laughter of the Garda Lake below
Sweet Catullus' all-but-island, olive-silvery Sirmio!

THE LAND

THE EAGLE

HE clasps the crag with crooked hands;
Close to the sun in lonely lands,
Ring'd with the azure world, he stands.

The wrinkled sea beneath him crawls;
He watches from his mountain walls,
And like a thunderbolt he falls.

THE OWL

I

WHEN cats run home and light is come,
    And dew is cold upon the ground,
And the far-off stream is dumb,
    And the whirring sail goes round,
    And the whirring sail goes round;
        Alone and warming his five wits,
        The white owl in the belfry sits.

When merry milkmaids click the latch,
    And rarely smells the new-mown hay,
And the cock hath sung beneath the thatch
    Twice or thrice his roundelay,
    Twice or thrice his roundelay;
        Alone and warming his five wits,
        The white owl in the belfry sits.

II

Thy tuwhits are lull'd, I wot,
  Thy tuwhoos of yesternight,
Which upon the dark afloat,
  So took echo with delight,
  So took echo with delight,
    That her voice, untuneful grown
    Wears all day a fainter tone.

I would mock thy chaunt anew;
  But I canot mimic it;
Not a whit of thy tuwhoo,
  Thee to woo to thy tuwhit,
  Thee to woo to thy tuwhit,
    With a lengthen'd loud halloo,
    Tuwhoo, tuwhit, tuwhit, tuwhoo-o-o!

THE THROSTLE

'Summer is coming, summer is coming.
  I know it, I know it, I know it.
Light again, leaf again, life again, love again!'
  Yes, my wild little Poet.

Sing the new year in under the blue.
  Last year you sang it as gladly.
'New, new, new, new!' Is it then *so* new
  That you should carol so madly?

'Love again, song again, nest again, young again,'
  Never a prophet so crazy!
And hardly a daisy as yet, little friend,
  See, there is hardly a daisy.

'Here again, here, here, here, happy year!'
  O warble unchidden, unbidden!
Summer is coming, is coming, my dear,
  And all the winters are hidden.

THE OAK

LIVE thy Life,
  Young and old,
Like yon oak,
Bright in spring,
  Living gold;
Summer-rich
  Then; and then
Autumn-changed,
Soberer-hued
  Gold again.
All his leaves
  Fallen at length,
Look, he stands,
Trunk and bough,
  Naked strength.

THE SNOWDROP

MANY, many welcomes,
February fair-maid,
Ever as of old time,
Solitary firstling,
Coming in the cold time,
Prophet of the gay time,
Prophet of the May time,
Prophet of the roses,
Many, many welcomes,
February fair-maid!

'FLOWER IN THE CRANNY'

FLOWER in the crannied wall,
I pluck you out of the crannies,
I hold you here, root and all, in my hand,
Little flower—but *if* I could understand
What you are, root and all, and all in all,
I should know what God and man is.

THE MAN

CROSSING THE BAR

SUNSET and evening star,
  And one clear call for me!
And may there be no moaning of the bar,
  When I put out to sea,

But such a tide as moving seems asleep,
  Too full for sound and foam,
When that which drew from out the boundless deep
  Turns again home.

Twilight and evening bell,
  And after that the dark!
And may there be no sadness of farewell,
  When I embark;

For tho' from out our bourne of Time and Place
  The flood may bear me far,
I hope to see my Pilot face to face
  When I have crost the bar.